Cultural Portrayals
of African Americans

Cultural Portrayals of African Americans

Creating an Ethnic/Racial Identity

Edited by
Janis Faye Hutchinson

BERGIN & GARVEY
Westport, Connecticut • London

Library of Congress Cataloging-in-Publication Data

Hutchinson, Janis Faye, 1953–
    Cultural portrayals of African Americans : creating an ethnic/racial identity / Janis Faye Hutchinson.
      p. cm.
    Includes bibliographical references (p.) and index.
    ISBN 0–89789–498–7 (alk. paper)
    1. Afro-Americans—Race identity—Congresses. 2. Afro-Americans in popular culture—Congresses. 3. Afro-Americans in mass media—Congresses. I. Title.
E185.625.H88   1997
305.896′073—dc20   96–46088

British Library Cataloguing in Publication Data is available.

Copyright © 1997 by Janis Faye Hutchinson

All rights reserved. No portion of this book may be reproduced, by any process or technique, without the express written consent of the publisher.

Library of Congress Catalog Card Number: 96–46088
ISBN: 0–89789–498–7

First published in 1997

Bergin & Garvey, 88 Post Road West, Westport, CT 06881
An imprint of Greenwood Publishing Group, Inc.

Printed in the United States of America

The paper used in this book complies with the Permanent Paper Standard issued by the National Information Standards Organization (Z39.48–1984).

10 9 8 7 6 5 4 3 2 1

Copyright Acknowledgments

The author and publisher gratefully acknowledge permission for the use of the following material:

Walker, S. S. and Kasamimanana, J. (1993). "Tarzan in the Classroom: How 'Education' Films Mythologize Africa and Miseducate Americans." *The Journal of Negro Education*. 62(1), 3–23. Reprinted by permission of *The Journal of Negro Education*.

This book is dedicated to our parents and families

Contents

Preface	ix
1. Introduction *Janis Faye Hutchinson*	1
2. The Resurgence of Genetic Hypotheses to Explain Social Behavior among Ethnic Minorities *Janis Faye Hutchinson*	5
3. Tarzan in the Classroom: How "Educational" Films Mythologize Africa and Miseducate Americans *Sheila S. Walker with Jennifer Rasamimanana*	27
4. Why Blacks Are Committed to Blackness *Rhett S. Jones*	49
5. Visual Images of the Postcolonial Blues on the Corner of Toulouse and Royal: Discord and Identity in *Songs of My People* *Helán E. Page with D. France Olivieira*	75
6. African-American Cultural Nationalism *Yvonne V. Jones*	113
7. Creating a Racial Identity *Janis Faye Hutchinson*	139

Index 151

About the Editor and Contributors 153

Preface

As members of the Association of Black Anthropologists, we often discuss the impetus for various interpretations of African-American history, culture, and experiences, especially within the field of anthropology. This effort can be troubling because often our experiences are labeled, categorized, and interpreted from a Eurocentric perspective. Such interpretations can sometimes lend themselves to a justification for slavery, subjugation, and a race-caste system in America. In so doing, any difference from the European *norm* is considered deviant. The question always seems to be phrased: Why are they different from Europeans? Such phraseology assumes deviation from an historical norm, and European culture and physique. If this is so, we must reevaluate the roots of portrayals of African Americans within the American sociocultural/scientific environment. We must also, then, examine the African-American response to such interpretations and imagery. This book endeavors to begin this process by investigating various ways African Americans are presented in printed media and in the visual arts, their conceptualization of black identity and cultural nationalism, and how hypotheses, i.e. genetic hypotheses, are formulated to explain their social behavior. This volume is based on papers presented in a symposium hosted by the Association of Black Anthropologists entitled *Managing the Past and Controlling the Future: the Role of Anthropologists*. The symposium was held at the national meeting of the American Anthropological Association in New Orleans, Louisiana, on November 29, 1990.

The goal of the symposium was to discuss various presentations and interpretations of African-American culture by non-African Americans and the impact of those portrayals on African-derived people. During the organization of the symposium, issues revolved around white co-optation and stereotypical interpretations of African-American culture. Topics at the conference centered on these issues. When I discussed the symposium with white colleagues, they were worried that the symposium might stress that whites should not study African Americans. My black colleagues were concerned about openly discussing negative interpretations and portrayals of black Americans by white Americans. In the final draft of papers another issue emerged, the creation of a positive racial identity by African Americans in response to negative portrayals of them by white America. This book presents examples of portrayals of blacks by blacks and by non-African Americans, and their reactions to such interpretations and images.

It is hoped that this book will contribute to an understanding of some of the major issues of cultural portrayals of African Americans and the creation of racial/ethnic identity. Hopefully, it will sensitize social scientists to the importance of "self" presentation of cultural aspects of one's own ethnic group and will provide suggestions on dealing with these issues in ways acceptable to African Americans in various arenas. The primary readers are expected to be social scientists, students, those concerned with race relations, ethnicity, and those enclaves involved in maintaining their cultural heritage within a larger and different cultural tradition.

I would like to thank Lesley Rankin-Hill for her help in organizing the symposium on *Managing the Past and Controlling the Future*. More than thanks to Wayne Young for listening to me talk about this book for three years. I also want to thank the contributors for their hard work, patience, commitment to the project, and for returning my phone calls.

CHAPTER 1

Introduction

Janis Faye Hutchinson

This volume examines portrayals of African Americans in various arenas: the media, biological hypotheses, visual images, black identity, and grass-roots cultural nationalist groups. Cultural presentations (in museum exhibits, the public media, and the academic and legal arena) of African Americans affect how others view them and how they view themselves. Along this line, such presentations determine the historical perspective for understanding minority cultures. This historical account influences not only how contemporary African Americans are viewed, but also how they will be seen in the future. The purpose of this book is to examine some of the problems in producing cultural portrayals of African Americans in the modern world and to determine the effect of these portrayals on minorities and nonminorities.

How should images of various ethnic groups be presented to the public, and who should control the presentation of these images? Most presentations of non-Western cultural groups in museums have been approached from the etic or outsider perspective. How has this approach affected both the popular and self-images of these groups? How should biocultural issues concerning minorities and non-Western communities be approached and reported? These questions are examined by investigating portrayals of African Americans in various arenas. Key points examined within this framework are: (1) there have been negative portrayals of ethnic minorities by nonminorities, (2) these negative portrayals have been internalized by ethnic minorities and nonminorities, and are perceived as true or correct representations, (3) such negative portrayals are usually myth or the product of historical racism, (4) there may be sociopolitical, economic, and academic motivations for negative portrayals of ethnic minorities, (5) negative portrayals affect race relations, and (6) negative cultural portrayals influence the in-group perception of racial/ethnic identity among African Americans.

Recently, academicians and nonacademicians were forced to consider their role and position on the previously discussed issues. For instance, Senator Inouye's Senate Bill S-1980 dealing with repatriation of human remains, grave goods and sacred objects of Native Americans forced archaeologists and physical anthropologists to reexamine their position and to take a stand on this issue. In general, it appears that academicians want to hold onto these materials and they cite various reasons for doing so. On the other hand, other professionals believe that these materials should be quickly examined and then reinterred. Professionals and government officials, and even Native Americans, disagree on this matter. Who should have the final word on it?

The African-American community also disagrees on the reburial issue. While some blacks believe that their ancestors should "rest in peace," others think that since so little is known about their ancestors, all information is welcome. How should the African-American community approach this issue and who should make the decision?

Other issues include the presentation of ethnic minorities in museums. This is considered a long-standing problem by people, such as Native Americans, who are typically portrayed in stereotypical ways in museums. For many years anthropologists believed that cultures evolved from the simple to the complex. Given enough time, "primitive" cultures would become civilized. It was believed that these cultures simply had not had enough time to progress to civilization. This view is reflected in many museum exhibits dealing with Native American and African-derived people.

Antagonisms have also arisen between people whose culture is portrayed and the "owners" of cultural artifacts (museums). For instance, in Canada the Lubicon Lake Cree boycotted an exhibition sponsored by a large oil company that was drilling on an unresolved land claim. As a result, some of the sponsors refused to lend artifacts for the exhibit. The Canadian Ethnology Society was on the side of the boycott, and academic anthropologists accused the museum of trying to keep Natives in the past by not allowing them to participate in the decision-making process and by exploiting them (Harrison and Trigger 1988). A more violent event occurred in Japan where the Sapporo Museum was bombed and statues were defaced. This was done in the name of Ainu liberation since presentations of Ainu in museums were denigrating. There is currently an Ainu revitalization movement aimed at consciousness-raising, preserving ethnocultural heritage, and improving living standards for the Ainu (Mitchell and Driedger 1978). Greater understanding between museum and academic anthropologists and the people being portrayed is needed, and a movement has been launched to change this situation. More and more ethnic people are developing their own museums, and museum directors are including representatives of ethnic minorities in their decision-making process.

The media have always been conveyors of identities, impacting readers', viewers', and listeners' perceptions of social phenomena. Among the people being portrayed, it can act as a confirmation of ethnic identity or a negative stereotype of the group. For individuals outside the representational group, it may provide the only characterization of other ethnic groups that these individuals will experience. To the outsider, these portrayals represent the behavior and culture of the group. Stereotypes of American Indians as savages, blacks as pimps and prostitutes and Mexicans as illegal immigrants have made an enormous impact on the way Americans view these ethnic groups.

Fernandez and Pedroza (1982) examined media presentations of undocumented immigrants from Mexico to the United States. The number of articles on the subject increased each year from 1972 to 1978. However, relatively few were written by Spanish-surnamed individuals and few used undocumented immigrants as sources of information. Information presented in articles during this period (in the *Los Angeles Times, New York Times, Washington Post*) was obtained from the Border Patrol, the Immigration and Naturalization Service, and politicians. News coverage of undocumented Mexican immigration was not balanced. However, the U.S. public accepted this biased information as an accurate reflection of social reality.

It also has been shown that images of U.S. cities presented in magazines, such as *National Geographic*, emphasize those elements connotative of U.S. superiority. Among blacks, the media have focused on the problems of the black family, teenage pregnancy, and drug abuse. This approach is superficial and blames the victim (Ladner 1986). Although the number of ethnic and racial minorities depicted in the media has risen since the 1960s, there has been little coverage of ethnic and minority life, and systemic disadvantages facing some groups are overlooked in the media (Raub 1988).

Questions such as who is an ethnic or who should possess artifacts from previous generations have always been controversial. For various reasons (compensation, census, federal assistance), the government has usually determined ethnicity. Should the government determine who is a Native American Indian or should it be determined by the Amerindian community? Also, who should control artifacts? Should these artifacts be given to the descendants in the area of discovery? Should a special museum be created in the area for them? Should the discoverer be allowed to keep them? This too is being scrutinized.

Some people may believe that it is inevitable for the "other" to portray ethnic minorities in negative ways. However, people can be sensitized to the perspective of the ethnic "other" and in some instances provide a more holistic record or history regarding the cultural patterns of ethnic minorities. The tone (attitude or mood) to be conveyed in the present work is that there can be an understanding of, if not identification with, ethnic "others" and that this understanding is important for the ethnic "self" and the ethnic "other." In response to these portrayals, How is racial identity created? While biology is involved, What makes a racial group feel a sense of group identity? This volume explores this issue using African Americans as a case study.

REFERENCES

Fernandez, C. and Pedroza, L.R. 1982. The border patrol and news media coverage of undocumented Mexican immigration during the 1970's: a quantitative content analysis in the sociology of knowledge. *California Sociologist* 5(2): 1–26.

Harms, V. 1990. The aims of the Museum for Ethnology: debate in the German-speaking countries. *Current Anthropology* 31(4): 457–463.

Harrison, J. and Trigger, B.G. 1988. The spirit sings and the future of anthropology. *Anthropology Today* 4(6): 6–9.

Ladner, J.A. 1986. Black women face the 21st century: major issues and problems. *Black Scholar* 17(5): 12–19.

Mitchell, J.F. and Driedger, L. 1978. Canadian ethnic folk art: an exploratory study in Winnipeg. *Ethnicity* 5(3): 252–265.

Raub, P. 1988. The *National Geographic Magazine's* portrayal of urban ethnicity: the celebration of cultural pluralism and the promise of social mobility. *Journal of Urban History* 14(3): 346–371.

Wittlin, A.S. 1970. *Museums: In Search of a Usable Future*. Cambridge, Mass: MIT Press.

Wolf, E.R. 1990. Facing power-insights, new questions. *American Anthropologist* 92(3): 586–596

CHAPTER 2

The Resurgence of Genetic Hypotheses to Explain Social Behavior among Ethnic Minorities

Janis Faye Hutchinson

Genetic theories are increasingly popular to explain sociocultural phenomena. Such theories have been used historically and in modern times to explain intellectual ability among racial/ethnic groups. In recent times Philippe Rushton used the r/k reproductive strategy to explain black/white/Asian patterns of criminality, intelligence, altruism, sex drive, behavioral restraint, and other socio-behavioral traits. Rushton's work provides an example of sociobiology, the ultimate biological reductionist model. Using an evolutionary model, sociobiologists believe they understand the genetics of behavior, although the specific genes producing behaviors (altruism, parental investment) are unknown. Such theories are used to explain social structure and cultural processes among ethnic minorities. As a result, "cultural achievements" among ethnic minorities are viewed as genetically determined, and the lack of "progress" is viewed in the same way. The origin and maintenance of racism within the scientific educational process is examined as a component in the production of "science."

INTRODUCTION

Why are biological explanations of social behavior among people of color prevalent today as in the past? This chapter focuses on the roots of this line of reasoning and provides a framework for understanding its current popularity in science. Since early historic times, Europeans created negative stereotypes of people of color. The motivation for these images was dominated by exploitative economic considerations. In order to legitimate European exploitation within the Christian world, those who were stereotyped were deemed less than human.

These stereotypes became the dominant images of people of color in the world and still influence our perceptions of them.

Negative perceptions of people of color were also legitimized by providing a "scientific" basis for preconceived ideas about non-Europeans. Today, science continues to rationalize and legitimize enculturated prejudice about people who are biologically different from those of European ancestry. This is done by generating hypotheses and framing data collection and analysis in such a way that the outcome is congruent with racist ideology. This chapter examines the evolution and maintenance of "racism in science." I use the phrase "racism in science" rather than "scientific racism" because the former provides a more salient perspective of the actual process of generating scientific knowledge about people of color in the Western world.

In the past two decades, there has been a resurgence of biological theories to explain human social behavior. This is increasingly evident in the academic community in terms of the number of articles and books on the subject, presentations at scientific meetings, specializations within traditional departments (not in behavioral genetics, but in sociobiology), the increased number of new journals on human social behavior which have a biological focus and the number of its proponents. While behavioral genetics has long been a focal area within biology, serious study of social relations within this branch of science is new. Although biological reductionism has been repeatedly debunked, it continues to be pervasive within the scientific community.

There may be a scientific seriousness in present biological theories because of current social inequalities that appear to be permanent (Alper 1977). Most Americans are concerned about crime, juvenile violence, child abuse, and other forms of antisocial or deviant behavior. We spend billions of dollars to incarcerate and rehabilitate individuals, and we impose the death penalty in order to permanently remove "deviants" from our ranks. Unfortunately, others take their place. We also provide treatment programs and therapy for spouse abusers, alcoholics, and the like, in an attempt to cure them of their deviancy. Despite these efforts, over a long period of time, deviancy continues to exist. There is a belief that since these efforts were not successful, deviancy is not environmentally determined but biological. In other words, these rehabilitation programs have not worked because deviant individuals are genetically programmed for this behavior. Therefore, social programs will not alleviate the problem. Proponents of biological determinism believe that the elimination of deviant behavior is basically out of our social control, except to reduce the reproduction of these individuals through incarceration and the death penalty. In the search for solutions to crime, defenders of the established order find comfort in the biological approach which blames crime on the individual rather than deficiencies in social, economic, and political institutions (Nassi and Abramowitz 1976).

In a plural, ethnocentric and racist environment such as ours, it is an easy psychological step to assume that certain behavioral differences between blacks and whites are genetically based, especially since we are continuously discovering genes for various abnormal behaviors such as schizophrenia. The belief that biology is responsible for mental and emotional differences between racial groups is an old idea.

A BRIEF HISTORY OF BIOLOGICAL DETERMINISM

In the 1500s Europeans began colonial exploration and encountered large numbers of Africans. When they saw dark skin, they already had preconceived ideas about blackness. For example, in the 16th century version of the Webster Dictionary, black was defined as dirty, evil, and darkness, whereas white, which they associated with themselves, was defined as pure, clean, good, and virginal (Williams and Morland 1976). Dark skin was distasteful to the European eye. Also, Europeans believed that African languages might not be languages at all; they also thought that their customs and appearances were so different that they could not be created in God's image. Because of these attributes, Europeans questioned whether Africans were human. Besides, they also encountered monkeys and apes and as far as they were concerned Africans could be another form of ape (Stepan 1982). The biology of Africans was seen as an indicator of their subhumanness and closeness to lower forms of animals. This being the case, the entire continent was theirs for exploitative colonization. The continent of Africa was unoccupied.

In the 17th century this idea was carried further by Joseph Lavater, the formulator of physiognomy. Lavater taught that by examining features of the face and the form of the body, one could judge the character and disposition of the individual (Davies 1955; McCoy 1985). For example, prognathism was viewed as an apelike characteristic. This trait indicated that your mental ability was on the level of an ape. He believed that form expressed the soul (Davies 1955).

Phrenologists were more specific in their approach. Phrenology is "the study of the faculties of the mind from the conformation of the skull" (Nassi and Abramowitz 1976:592). Franz Joseph Gall, the developer of this concept, observed friends, students, as well as people in mental institutions and attempted to associate the size of certain parts of the skull with specific mental abilities. Gall and later his student, Spurzheim divided the skull into components such as lovingness, combativeness, sexamity, friendship, and secretiveness. After examining the heads of some of his most quarrelsome companions, Gall identified the area designated as combativeness. This area was confirmed by observing this region on the head of a quarrelsome lady acquaintance. The trait for acquisitiveness was just behind the temple because he knew two pickpockets with prominent bumps in this area (McCoy 1985; McLaren 1981).

Phrenologists advocated a correspondence between specific crimes and contours on the head. They believed that certain crimes such as theft and murder were associated with organs for combativeness, secretiveness, and destructiveness (Nassi and Abramowitz 1976). Thus, they attempted to use biology to understand behavior.

In the 1800s, this process became "more scientific." George Samuel Morton studied medicine in Edinburgh from 1820 to 1823 and while there he attended meetings of the Phrenological Society (Erickson 1979). The meetings evidently made a lasting impression on him because fifteen years later he wrote Combe, a disciple of Gall, to introduce himself, expressed interest in phrenology, and told him about his forthcoming book, *Crania Americana* (1839). Morton told Combe that the book would be of interest to phrenologists and that the facts in his book would support the basic principles and details of phrenology (Erickson 1979). Morton implied that *Crania Americana* was a test of phrenology, and he considered the hypothesis confirmed, that is, that there is a correspondence between mental ability and cranial development as expounded by phrenologists (Morton 1839).

Scientists like Paul Broca and Morton calculated cranial capacity and substituted these measurements for prior visual inspection. Europeans were the standard, and others were considered deviants from this norm. Therefore, similarity to European measurements meant higher intelligence. During this period, measurements were used to determine criminality, intellectual ability, and personality. Craniometry could be used to explain anything (Gould 1981).

Cesare Lombroso put forth the doctrine of criminal atavisim which holds that criminals are an "atavistic reversal" or a throwback to a primitive form of human. After examining the skulls and brains of criminals, Lombroso was convinced that criminals exhibited certain primitive characteristics such as receding chins, woolly hair, and lobeless and small ears. He used metric and morphological data to support his contention (Nassi and Abramowitz 1976). Although the doctrine was seriously flawed, it was an influential scientific theory of crime through the early 20th century (Gould 1981).

After Darwin published *Origin of the Species* (1859), scientists such as his cousin Francis Galton applied Darwin's concept of natural selection to societies. Social Darwinism states that, similar to species, there is competition between societies and survival or dominance of the fittest societies. Social Darwinists believed that competition was inherent and that the society which prevailed was destined to conquer and dominate other societies (Gossett 1965). It was manifest destiny. It was God's will, and those who ruled were meant to be rulers. Social Darwinism justified classism, sexism and racism. In the 1920s, the theory of social Darwinism was applied to humans in the eugenics movement.

After W.W.II scientists were concerned with adaptation to various environments. Studies on adaptation to cold, heat, stress, and altitude were predominant (Baker 1958; Livingstone 1958). Environmental influences on physiology were the focus, and behavior was viewed as the product of the complex interaction between environmental factors and culture.

Still, some researchers clung to the old paradigm of biological determinism. For example, in 1962 Carlton S. Coon published *The Origins of Races* in which he espoused the view that each race evolved from *Homo erectus* in the local area. For instance, Africans evolved from *Homo erectus* in Africa, Asians from *Homo erectus* in Asia, and Europeans from those forms in Europe. This is a quasi-polygenesis view of evolution and is similar to the current multiregional model of human evolution (Wolpoff 1985). However, Coon stated that when Africans evolved there was no gene flow and that Africans did not evolve as fast as Europeans. Therefore African culture, intellect and personality were not as fully evolved as those of Europeans, but in time they would evolve further.

CURRENT EXAMPLES OF BIOLOGICAL DETERMINISM

The belief that biology is the primary determinant of behavior continues to the present. Three current examples of biological reductionism are Rushton's r/k strategy of racial differences, sociobiology, and intellectual ability as measured by IQ.

J. Philippe Rushton's r/k Strategy of Racial Variation

Rushton explains human variation in terms of differential k theory. In evolutionary biology, k refers to one end of the reproductive continuum in which organisms are characterized by the production of few offspring with a large investment of energy in each. The k strategy is the maximum carrying capacity of the species in a stable and predictable environment. At the other end of the continuum is the r strategy in which organisms produce a large number of offspring but invest little energy in any one. According to population biology, r is the maximal intrinsic reproductive rate in a population temporarily free from resource limitations. It is hypothesized that this strategy evolved in an unstable and unpredictable environment (Rushton 1985).

While r/k strategy was developed to make comparisons *between species*, Rushton uses it to examine variations in life history, personality, and social behavior *within* the human species. Rushton argues that many personality and social behaviors are heritable and that these characteristics are associated with r/k strategies (Rushton 1985, 1988a, 1988b). Using the work of Eisenberg (1981), Rushton notes that the mammalian radiations showed an increasing trend toward k. Rushton (1985) observes that:

competition over resource bases could select for long life, small litters and trends toward iteroparity, which, if the resource base then varied from year to year, could select for increased percentage of life span spent in social learning. This in turn, could lead to high encephalization, with concomitant central nervous system growth in a long gestation period and continuing development after birth, which then could select for delayed sexual maturation and the creation of a complex interdependent social grouping with high degrees of altruism. (Rushton 1985:443)

Drawing on Lovejoy's work (1981), Rushton points out that humans are the most k of all the primates. He states: "As Lovejoy (1981) pointed out, the order primates display a *scala naturae* from lemur to macaque to gibbon to chimp to man, in which there is a trend toward k with prolonged life span prolonged gestation, single births, successively longer periods between pregnancies and developmental delay" (Rushton 1985:444).

Rushton believes that some humans are more k than others, that this variance is under genetic influence, and that k behavior is associated with an array of personality traits resulting from natural selection (Rushton 1985, 1988a). Based on these strategies, he states that certain predictions can be made in terms of life history traits, social behavior, and physiological functioning. For instance, "The more k the family, the more stable it will be, the less likely it is to have dizygotic twins (a measure of 'litter size'), the greater the spacing between births, the fewer the total number of offspring, the lower the rate of infant mortality and the better developed the parental care" (Rushton 1985:445).

In terms of personality and social behavior: "The more k the person, the higher the intelligence, the more altruism manifested, the greater the law-abidingness, the lower the overall activity level and the lower the sex drive" (Rushton 1985:445).

Like Morton and Broca, Rushton equates cranial capacity and brain weight with increased intelligence. Rushton (1988a) provides calculations of cranial capacity from observations by Coon (1982) and Howells (1973). Also, based on the work of Jensen (1969), Rushton assumes that standardized IQ tests are measures of intelligence and that there is a genetically based difference between racial groups. He totally discounts cultural biases in the tests and downplays the influence of environmental variables on IQ test results.

Based on this information, Rushton ranked groups. In terms of k, higher SES > lower SES and Mongoloids > Caucasoids > Negroids (Rushton 1985, 1988a). In other words, people in higher SES and Mongoloids are more k oriented. He stated that "the most efficient unit of analysis . . . is the higher order concept of race, within which cluster the different ethnic groups and ultimately, individuals" (Rushton, 1988a:1009). He does not explain why this is the most efficient unit of analysis. We can only infer that he wanted his results to focus on these categories.

Rushton (1985) argues that there must be a genetic basis for the within-species differences in social behaviors. However, there is no reason to assume that this is so. In any investigative research, the most parsimonious theory is given more credence. The r/k strategy does not fit this criterion. First, gene flow connects us as a species. Even if these personality traits are genetically based, there is no reason to assume that altruism, intelligence, pair-bonding, and the like are more prevalent in one group than another. Any environment could select for these traits. There is no evidence associating these social traits with particular environments in which natural selection operated. What selection pressures would create differences between racial groups? Rushton states that he will "leave in abeyance" this question (Rushton 1985).

Rushton uses data that support his hypothesis without considering the validity of alternate explanations. For example, he notes that while African Americans constitute only 12% of the U.S. population, they account for 48% of the prison population. He reports that Chinese and Japanese in North America have a lower incidence of crime than people of European or African ancestry (Rushton 1985). Rushton only examines street crime. If he included white-collar crime, his results would be quite different. It is evident that environmental factors can explain these differences. However, Rushton already decided that differences are due to genetic variation.

According to Gabor and Roberts (1990) Rushton did not address errors in his data that they identified in his previous publications. Of course, these errors are always in the direction supportive of Rushton's hypothesis. They stated that:

He is also remarkably silent about the evidence we have provided from alternative sources of data: victimization surveys and self-reports. This evidence indicates that official crime statistics often inflate racial differences.

Furthermore, Rushton does not attempt to explain the very substantial within-race differences in criminality across cultures and over time. . . . Nor does he attempt to reconcile with his views the fact that the homicide rate, for example, in Caribbean countries such as the Bahamas and Jamaica, as well as among African-Americans, exceeds that in most African countries, where the black population is more racially pure. (Gabor and Roberts 1990:337)

Lastly, Rushton does not address the fact that these racial groups differ in other ways besides genetics. Cultural, social, and economic differences between the racial groups could explain his findings.

Sociobiology

Rushton's work provides an example of sociobiology. Sociobiology is similar to certain historical explanations of human behavior which considered a single factor, biology, to be the primary causative agent of behavior. Thus, biological reductionism is the unifying feature between these historical explanations and sociobiology. Sociobiology was introduced by E.O. Wilson (1975a) in *Sociobiology: The New Synthesis*. Wilson defined sociobiology as "the systematic study of the biological basis of all social behavior, including the evolution of social behaviors and their relationship to genetic change" (Wilson 1975a:4). Henry Harpending and colleagues (1987:127) redefined sociobiology as "the study of human behavior based on a Darwinian paradigm." The focus of this definition is on the effect of natural selection on behavior, and researchers may or may not be concerned with genes. It is an attempt to explain interpersonal interactions and social behavior as the product of natural selection. However, all behaviors within a species do not appear to be adaptive. It is these behaviors that are of primary concern to the sociobiologist.

Sociobiologists explain social behavior in terms of maximization of inclusive fitness. In other words, people try to increase the proportion of their genes passed on to the next generation not only by helping their own children but also by being altruistic. They can do so in two ways. They can make it possible for other family members to increase their survivorship and therefore pass on a percentage of genes to the next generation that are similar to theirs (kin selection), or they can help a stranger to survive in the hope that it will be reciprocated and thereby increase their own survivorship and fitness (reciprocal altruism). Those who exhibit altruistic behaviors are going to be selected for in the population and will therefore have higher survivorship and fertility.

Sociobiologists do not attempt to explain just any type of human behavior. They focus on social relations such as parental care, bonding, aggression, and altruism. Sociobiology attempts to explain complex social interactions in a modern industrialized world without considering cultural history, enculturation, and the socialization processes. Instead, they postulate genes to account for human social relations. Washburn (1978) and others note that at present a direct link between specific genes and social behavior has not been found (Gould and Lewontin 1979). There is no evidence linking human social behavior with particular genes missing, nor are there any data indicating that social behavior is genetically based. Specific types of social behaviors do not aggregate within families and do not follow predictable patterns of degree of genetic relatedness. Within families, members may or may not be aggressive, criminal, or loving. Using contemporary models of genetic transmission, empirical data do not indicate that social relationships are genetically determined. Since a link between genetics and social relations is lacking, "sociobiology may be useful and illuminating, or reductionist, racially biased, and absurd" (Washburn 1978:36). Without a link between social behavior and genetics, natural selection cannot be invoked to explain such phenomenon (Caplan 1984).

Often, sociobiologists formulate questions in such a way that any legitimate answer validates the social preference (Gould 1981). A major question asked by sociobiologists is: "Why has natural selection favored certain forms of social behavior such as parental care, self-sacrificing assistance to siblings, or the formation of monogamous mating bonds?" (Irons 1981:148). In the sociobiology paradigm, social behavior is viewed as the product of natural selection. Sociobiologists assume that natural selection favors certain social traits and that researchers work within this domain. However, the first question should be: has natural selection favored certain forms of *social* behavior? While traveling on the *H.M.S. Beagle*, Darwin gathered data indicating that forms differed from one environment to the next, and he conducted excavations showing that organism varied over time. *Then* he considered possible mechanisms that could create this variation. Sociobiologists appear to be starting at this point with the mechanism, without first documenting the idea that social behavior has a certain distributional pattern (Irons 1981). Instead of creating a problem, Darwin was presented with a problem to solve, variation. Sociobiologists have not gathered data demonstrating an association between certain social behaviors and varying environments in which selection would occur. Populations have existed in differing environments long enough for behavioral-genetic adaptations to occur, if they are going to appear. Instead, what we find is a wide range of social relations in diverse environments.

Sociobiologists select certain aspects of human social behavior to reify. For instance, they discuss various social interactions such as a man jumping on a grenade to save his friends, a mother risking her life to protect her child, or doctors risking infection while working in leprosy colonies. Then a common feature, self-sacrificing, is abstracted from these actions and categorized as altruistic behavior (Rose 1979). Rose writes that sociobiologists "abstracted reified aspects of a social interaction into uniform qualities of an individual participant in that interaction" (p. 282). The fact that these behaviors occur meant that they could be grouped. Sociobiologists chose altruism as the umbrella term to explain these actions (Rose 1979). Once the concept of altruistic behavior was developed, they looked for the source of the behavior within the individual. This type of reification is similar to that of phrenologists who atomized behavior into discrete categories and then sought the source of the behavior from within the individual.

This approach easily reverts to what Gould (1980b) terms the "just-so stories." Storytelling is based on maximization-of-inclusive-fitness and kin selection (Gould 1980b). If stories could be rejected, then alternative explanations could be examined. However, these stories are never rejected due to lack of evidence or contradictory evidence. Such a definable rejection is not possible because (1) it is replaced by another adaptive story that is similar to the first and (2) criteria for acceptance of a story is loose. Gould writes that "sociobiologists are still telling speculative stories, still hitching without evidence to one potential star among many, still using mere consistency with natural selection as a criterion of acceptance" (Gould 1980b:260), "and consider their work done when they concoct a plausible story" (Gould and Lewontin 1979:588).

Rose (1979) discussed what he refers to as "just-suppose" stories. He believes that sociobiologists always begin explaining the presence of a trait by stating: "just suppose" social traits are genetically determined. What would be the consequences? Then examples that fit the model (inclusive fitness) are used to explain the social behavior. Sociobiologists ignore the fact that other models also fit the data (Rose 1979). Rose stated that "there is no sort of situation to which one cannot get a fit granted enough suppositions about genes for this or that piece of behavior and some other genetic properties like dominance or partial expressivity" (Rose 1979:284). The sociobiological model is so comprehensive that any new facts are compatible with it. It has become the ultimate reductionist model (Rose 1979).

By quantifying genetic relatedness and presumed correlated behavior-genetic relatedness, the reified quality, for example, altruism, is quantified. Quantification is always seen as being more scientific than qualitative analysis (Rose 1979). Such quantification is an attempt to make sociobiology scientific. The problem with this is that no matter what number you compute, you cannot be sure what the number means. Statistical significance does not necessarily mean biological or sociological significance. Also, we do not know that the fixed abstraction represents the social action. What good is it to study parental investment and devise a formula which shows that some individuals are more altruistic than others, if we do not know that parental investment is an example of altruistic behavior (Rose 1979).

The issue to discuss is the fact that sociobiology is biological determinism with a new name. Then, the problem to resolve is the recognition of this discipline as simply a new version of an old approach, craniometry, that still has numerous fallacies. At this point in our scientific development we do not know enough about the genetics of physical characteristics and cannot begin to identify genes that determine social behavior, if they exist. Some researchers will say, "well, suppose there is a genetic basis for social interactions, then you should have certain expectations." If the expectations are not met then they say that either they are missing information or they provide another biological story. This is not science. It is an attempt to promote one's own biased ideas about social interactions under the guise of science.

Intelligence

Intellectual differences between racial/ethnic groups and social classes have long been a subject of debate. A scientific approach in this debate began in 1905 when Binet and Simon developed the Metrical Scale of Intelligence. In 1904 Alfred Binet was commissioned by the Ministry of Public Education in Paris to devise a scale that would identify children whose poor performance indicated that special education was needed. The purpose of the scale was to identify children with learning disability or those mildly retarded (Gould 1981). Binet (1908) stated that the scale should be used to identify individuals of inferior grades of intelligence. He did not intend for it to be used on "normal pupils" (Gould 1981).

The scale itself consisted of diverse activities. By using such a mixture, Binet hoped to abstract the general potential of a child with a single score. Later, Binet assigned an age to these varying tasks. Binet wrote: "The scale, properly speaking, does not permit the measure of intelligence, because intellectual qualities are not superposable, and therefore cannot be measured as linear surfaces are measured" (Binet 1905, in Gould 1981:151). The scale is an average of many performances, and Binet warned against reifying it as an entity. He did not want the test to be used as a label, but rather as an identifier of "underachievers." However, the IQ test was born, in 1912 when W. Stern, a German physiologist, argued that Binet's mental age should be divided by chronological age (Gould 1981). It was then transferred to the United States where it underwent enormous modifications and has since been used as a measure of "intelligence."

Charles Spearman believed that what Binet discovered in his IQ test was g. Using a version of factor analysis, Spearman computed a factor, termed g, which he believed was the innate essence of intelligence. He considered it the underlying structure of intelligence. For Spearman, g showed that intelligence is a single, measurable entity. This provided the theoretical justification for theorists who believe that IQ is genetically based. Now they could measure intelligence, because they could compute g (Gould 1981).

In contemporary times Arthur Jensen has been the major proponent of inherent differences in intellectual ability between the races and classes. Jensen's hereditarian view of IQ is based on g, which he believes is a measure of intelligence. He did not try to define intelligence, but stated that the important fact is that it can be measured. He writes that "intelligence, like electricity, is easier to measure than to define. And if the measurements bear some systematic relationship to other data, it means we can make meaningful statements about the phenomenon we are measuring"(Jensen 1969:5).

Jensen also used heritability estimates as a measure of the genetic component of IQ and he determined that the heritability of intelligence is high (85%). Jensen operated under the misguided assumption that genes and environment are completely separate and therefore easily identifiable and measurable. To the contrary, there is interaction which makes isolation of the components difficult.

Jensen (1969) believed that since racial groups have been geographically and socially "isolated" from other such groups for many generations, there are certain differences in gene frequencies (and consequently differences in phenotypes with high heritability). According to Jensen, there is no reason to think that mental abilities are not included in this scenario. He concluded that "there seems to be little question that racial differences in genetically conditioned behavioral characteristics, such as mental abilities, should exist, just as physical differences"(Jensen 1969:80).

Jensen (1969) examined IQ scores between blacks and whites. Based on data in the literature, Jensen concluded that blacks test about 1 standard deviation (15 IQ points) lower than the average for whites. The difference, states Jensen, is due not to discrimination or inequality in education, but to genetic differences. Jensen (1972) also attempted to show that social and class differences have an hereditary basis. The lower socioeconomic position of some groups, he said, is due to their lowered intellectual capacity and education, and other pedagogics will not rectify this situation (Jensen 1969).

Richard Herrnstein and Charles Murray's *The Bell Curve* rehashes the proposal in earlier studies that IQ is a quantifiable measure of intelligence. They believe that there are intellectual differences between racial groups and do not consider inherent problems with this proposition. IQ is not equivalent to intelligence. IQ, which is used to measure intelligence, is an achieved and not an inherent score. The IQ score tells us how well an individual performs relative to a standard population. The standard is usually a population of European ancestry. IQ tests demonstrate achieved learning and not the potential for learning. Therefore, it can only be used to determine how much an individual has learned relative to the achieved learning of the standard European population used as the reference.

Environmental factors must be assessed in terms of interactive effects with the genotype. Views about education and taking tests affect how one performs on examinations. Also, nutrition is extremely important in the development of the central nervous system. These factors are ignored or considered unimportant in these models.

The generation and exploration of "scientific" hypotheses do not occur in a vacuum; rather, they must be examined and interpreted within a racial world context. "Scientists" are born and raised through a sociocultural based socialization process and like nonscientists, they are vulnerable to folk beliefs and folk science. Racism can have an enormous impact on scientific inquiry.

THE DEVELOPMENT OF A RACIST PERSPECTIVE

Biological determinism is the foundation of racism. Why is biological determinism maintained in modern times? In particular, why is racism a part of scientific endeavors? Allport (1954) suggested that early in life negative attitudes may be "caught" rather than "taught." Once caught, it is difficult to change. Katz stated that "The relative imperviousness of adult prejudice to the effects of conflicting evidence and experience strongly suggests that predispositions acquired at early developmental levels may form the irrational but potent foundation for racism" (1976:125). In numerous studies Katz showed that racism is learned in early childhood (Katz 1973; Katz and Zalk 1974; Katz et al. 1975). Studies suggest that many children acquire racial attitudes at around 3 or 4 years of age. At this time children make differential responses to skin color and other racial cues. In nursery school children develop ethnic attitudes that help them to establish self-identity. A child learns which group he does and does not belong to and also associates these groups with negative and positive feelings (Katz 1976). Proshansky (1966) concluded that racial awareness is well established by 6 years of age.

Goodman's (1952) classic study of children's attitudes illustrates the entrenched racial attitudes of children. Goodman found that children used words related to racism, although the feelings were not yet present. One 4 year old summed up their views: "The people that are white, they can go up. The people that are brown, they have to go down."

Although social scientists agree that the acquisition of racial attitudes is complex and multi-influenced, factors related to racial attitude can be partitioned into single determinants. Katz (1976) reviews these determinants. Direct instruction is the most common-sense source of transmission of racial attitudes. Parents and relatives transmit their attitudes to offspring, and the timing of transmission may be important. For instance, early types of impressions may be more difficult to alleviate than later exposures. Reinforcement of a child's positive and negative attitudes by adults or peers is another mechanism for learning prejudice.

Williams and Morland (1976) suggested that racial awareness prior to 3 years of age may be related to nonverbal cues such as day and night. In a number of articles, Williams suggests that fear of the dark among children may be generalized to dark-skinned people (Williams 1966; Williams et al. 1971; Williams and Morland 1976). Williams tested people in a variety of cultures and found that most preferred light to dark colors (Williams and Morland 1976). Linguistic symbolism and cultural expectations may reinforce racial stereotypes (Williams 1966).

Another theoretical mechanism for the acquisition of racial attitudes is an authoritarian personality structure. Here, prejudice in children is due to being reared by harsh and rigid parents. According to this model, children must submit to harsh and uncompromising parents and are never permitted to express resultant hostility toward them. As a defensive mechanism, the child identifies with the authoritarian parent and is aggressive toward out-group persons since they cannot express hostility toward the in-group parents (Katz 1976).

Allport (1954) suggested a cognitive aspect of racial attitudes. He states that prejudiced individuals overcategorize and believe that all people in a category behave in the same way and have the same traits. Overcategorization does not change because of contradictory and new information and is not easily reversible. This is related to the authoritarian theory in terms of why children raised in rigid households jump the gun, overgeneralize and resist changing categories once they are formed.

Lastly, it is widely believed that the most basic prerequisite to racism is perceptual difference. Allport (1954) suggested that physical differences imply real differences to children. Strangeness increases the development of negative attitudes.

Racialization of the Education Process

According to Kuhn (1962), "scientific communities" determine what paradigms to study and when to discard one paradigm for another. The social, political, economic and cultural ideologies of "scientific communities" determine which paradigms are more acceptable. Kuhn (1962) discussed the concept of tacit knowledge. This is adherence to a paradigm because it is acquired through exposure to the literature and education without completely understanding why this paradigm is more acceptable in the scientific community. In what Kuhn (1962) terms normal science, there are no debates concerning the course of research strategies and concerning the worth of the hypotheses. To be scientific "is simply to be a member of a community which shares a nest of commitments" (Kuhn 1962:100).

To understand why a claim is considered valid, you must understand the social conditions in which the claim is made (Laudan 1977). Milic (1984) states that the social functions of knowledge and ideas are: (1) practico-technical, (2) socio-integrative, and (3) a concerned formation of worldview. In the first function, the practico-technical, ideas and skills are used to perform various roles in the social division of labor (such as education, administration, and health care). There is a practico-technical knowledge that each professional group learns for its professional practice. The socio-integrative function of knowledge is to justify the social order. This can be accomplished on a global level by justifying the entire social order and by justifying social statuses, rights, privileges, organization of activities and how they are carried out. Lastly, knowledge can organize worldviews and self-consciousness through the practico-technical and socio-integrative functions (Milic 1984).

To understand the sociology of knowledge, Milic (1984) stated that we need systematic examinations of the relationship between society and science in terms of (1) internal relations, (2) economic, political, legal, and other associations within society, and (3) the position of the scientists within the class system of the society. Examination of academia, training, and scientific publication processes are also necessary if we are to understand why one paradigm is more popular than others (Milic 1984).

In academic institutions, students are taught to think about science in a certain manner. In this way, knowledge is diffused and the paradigm remains popular. The fact that some individuals at large institutions collaborate and are able to publish more means that they have a greater impact on the scientific community. The "Matthew effect" in which eminent scientists are more rapidly and easily published is also an important mode of paradigm transmission (Milic 1984). Over time, collective activity can have the appearance of objectivity (Fuller 1987). The proliferation of publications on sociobiology in respected journals gives the impression of universal acceptance in the scientific community. Such reading by new students entering the field provides the education for acceptance of the paradigm without knowledge of its correctness or appropriateness for investigating human social behavior.

In classrooms, individuals are treated differentially, although, according to the law, there is equal opportunity. Gender and ethnic differences between student and teacher result in subtle differences in teaching approach, interaction between student and teacher, classroom experiences, and opportunities to excel. While differential interaction between student-teachers may be considered to be due to cultural differences, the interaction is founded on preconceived and enculturated ideas about intellectual capability and future success of the student.

All knowledge is interest-laden and has a social root. Three types of groups have an interest in the acceptance of certain knowledge: (1) motivators who propose the knowledge in the hope that they will benefit from it, (2) benefiters, who benefit from the claim of the knowledge and (3) users, who make use of the claim in order to propose additional knowledge claims (Fuller 1987). Biological reductionists can fall into all three groups.

Fuller (1987:155) stated that "granting epistemic warrant is a covert form of distributing power." If certain knowledge had equal benefit for all rational beings, then it would have no net effect on the distribution of power. Knowledge would be value-neutral if there was equal access to it and equal benefit from it. If any rational being with a modicum of training could participate in the acquisition of knowledge, the quality of knowledge produced would be increased and value biases would be purged. There would not be what Fuller

(1987) called a "cult of expertise." If people are not part of the expert group, they have to depend on them for certain knowledge and must bow to their authority (Fuller 1987). If this occurs, social policymaking is linked to the sociology of knowledge (Mannheim 1940). It is then important to understand why the expert group determines what is appropriate for people outside their group. Who benefits from the knowledge claim? This is important when examining biological determinism because of the social impact of such inquiries. Biological determinists seem to believe that social policymaking is outside of their purview, although they claim that, for instance, sociobiology will encompass the social sciences which includes policymaking.

Fuller (1987) discusses the norms of scientific practice which function as tacit civil codes. Scientists are constrained by these codes, but such codes cannot prevent individuals from couching unwarranted claims in a manner that conforms to the codes and that are therefore acceptable to scientists (Fuller 1987). For instance, Cyril Burt's findings were accepted for a long time because the presentation of his results conformed to scientific inquiry. After a number of different studies, it is expected that the fradulent or manipulative research will be discovered. Nonetheless, results from such studies can have long-term effects on scientific thinking. The tacit civil code provides what is supposed to happen in the research pursuit, given the norms of the discipline. However, reproduction of knowledge in articles, books, and the like does not demonstrate how knowledge is actually produced. For instance, it does not tell us what led up to the production of the knowledge (Fuller 1987).

RACISM IS ADAPTIVE

Given that biological determinism has been dismissed each time it has arisen, why has it reappeared in various forms such as Rushton's r/k strategy? There are no unambiguous facts to support the reappearance of biological determinism. No new information has been found to replace previous findings that refuted biological determinism. Support appears to be related to social and political influences (Gould 1977). Gould (1977) wrote that biological determinism has reemerged because of "pedestrian pursuits of high royalties for best sellers to pernicious attempts to reintroduce racism as respectable science. Their common denominator must lie in our current malaise" (Gould 1977:239).

Gould (1977) stated that it is easy to blame our ancestors for our current violence, and it is easier to blame the poor for being poor than to find fault in the economic system of our society. "And how convenient an argument for those who control government and, by the way, provide the money that science requires for its very existence" (Gould 1977:239).

Since racism is learned as part of social and educational processes, it is difficult to unlearn. It is similar to the biological concept of developmental adaptation. In this instance, if an individual experiences physiological stressors during growth and development, it is permanent for the individual. For instance, people at high altitudes chronically suffer from hypoxia. One way the body responds to this physiological stressor is to enlarge the right ventrical of the heart so that more blood and hemoglobin are transported to the tissue. The enlarged heart is permanent for the individual who experienced hypoxia during critical periods of growth. Similarly, racial attitudes are learned during the growth process. Early experiences can have lasting effects on racial attitudes. Racism is therefore developmental. Unlike developmental acclimatization, "developmental racism," at least theoretically, can be lost or unlearned. But since the acquisition of racial attitudes is part of our early social development, it is extremely difficult to unlearn in adulthood. Racist attitudes are then passed from one generation to the next through the process of enculturation.

In American society, a major reason why racism is difficult to alleviate is denial. Racism is not only politically incorrect, but also expression of it in the form of discrimination is illegal, under certain circumstances. In order to unlearn a process one has to accept the fact that there is something to unlearn. One must self-identify with racists and attempt to reduce the level of negative racial thinking and its expression on an individual level. It is easier and adaptive to deny the problem because one can continue to be politically correct.

Racism is also adaptive for the dominant group because it maintains the status quo. In 1620 Francis Bacon codified the Renaissance belief that the goal of science is the attainment of power. According to Bacon, the purpose of science is to control and dominate the environment in which we live (Bacon 1955). While it is obvious that science is used to alter conditions of our lives, it is less apparent that science serves the interests of the dominant group (to control the environment and the people in them). This was done by theoreticians such as Aristotle, Aquinas and Locke who created theories of human nature to rationalize their societies and to maintain the status quo (Alper 1977).

To maintain the Greek system Socrates ranked individuals; he divided people into rulers, auxiliaries and craftsmen based on inherent mythological characteristics. Socrates fabricated a tale to make people believe that they should accept the rank ascribed to them. He asserted that even if the current population did not accept the myth, it would become a part of tradition in later generations. In that way, future generations would accept the status quo (Gould 1981).

Plato also ranked individuals by inborn worth using a dialectic approach. Much later, biological determinism was used to validate Plato's story. The argument of biological determinists has not changed since the time of Plato: "that social and economic roles accurately reflect the innate construction of people" (Gould 1981:20). The difference now is that biological determinism purports to be based on firm scientific principles. It provides a legitimacy that the theoreticians and philosophers lacked (Alper 1977).

This type of science, biological determinism, benefits people in power. Unfortunately, researchers are not heeding Santayana who said that those who do not know history are doomed to repeat it (George Santayana in Nassi and Abramowitz 1976:591). Also, those who know history may elect to repeat it (Nassi and Abramowitz 1976).

DISCUSSION

Since humans are animals, biology constrains all phenotypic expressions. For instance, stature, maturation, aging, death, and so on fall within genetically determined range. All biologists recognize that genes set limits on the range of animal variability. However, genes do not provide blueprints for exact replicas. Biological determinists, especially sociobiologists, believe that the range of variability for human social behavior is predictable because individuals possess certain genes. In this sense, the range of behavioral variability for the individual is narrow, being predetermined by the genes of the possessor. While biological determinists consider behavior to have a narrow range of variability because people possess certain genes, critics have a broader perspective. They view genes in terms of genetic potential, rather than equating them with a predetermined phenotypic outcome (Gould 1981). The environment can change genetic orientation. It is this interaction which determines the outcome.

While all animals operate within biological constraints, phenotypic expression is influenced by the interaction of diverse environments with the genotype. The same genotype can produce a different phenotypic expression in differing environments. For instance, an individual may have the genetic potential to have the intelligence of Einstein. However, if the individual is raised in a cardboard box with little intellectual stimulation, this genetic potential will not likely be realized. We tend to want to see evolution as progressive and to place ourselves at the top. We like to attribute all traits that we dislike to genetic endowment from our ape-like ancestors, while traits we cherish are considered unique to us and due to our rationality (Gould 1977).

An example of this process is illustrated by psychologists. Those psychologists who subscribe to the idea that behavior is determined use a methodology called orientation on the individual. Based on this perspective, if an individual is unhappy, poor or a criminal, it is his fault and not the social system. Caplan and Nelson (1973) examined studies of blacks in the United States and revealed that 82% of the studies found that problems in the black population are due to their personal shortcomings while 16% showed that the social system contributed to their problems. Such collective activity gives the appearance of objectivity and correctness. Again, the problem is within the individual without examining the socio-political and economic history of the phenomena.

Learning during growth and development is ignored in biological determinism. For instance, concerning sex roles Wilson (1975b:35) writes that "even with identical education and equal access to all professions, men are likely to continue to play a disproportionate role in political life, business and science." According to Wilson (1975b), sex-role behavioral traits are inherent and unchangeable. There are numerous explanatory models of role differences between the sexes ranging from biological to socialization models (Brown 1957; Hartley 1959; Lynn 1962; Mead 1928; Millett 1971; Tiger 1969). For instance, Ullian (1981) provides a structural developmental approach. She suggested that increased levels of aggression and power-seeking reported among boys reflect their effort to give psychological expression to their perceived gender characteristics. Studies of children between 4 and 7 years of age indicate that these children distinguish masculinity and femininity along such dimensions as size, strength, depth of voice, body and facial hair, and capacity to bear children (Kagan 1956; Kohlberg 1966). When children between these ages are asked to describe women, they say that they are small, gentle, physically powerless, pretty, have high-pitched voices, and are future mothers. In contrast, men are viewed as larger, more powerful, having facial and body hair, and a deep voice (Ullian 1981).

Since children are unable to distinguish between psychological and physical attributes, they conclude that women are by nature nicer because their skin is softer or because their voices are nicer; since they are physically weaker, they cry more easily. In addition, girls believe their sex is more capable of rearing children because boys cannot give birth. Interviews with young girls indicate that they believe that there is already a baby inside them, that the stork will bring the baby to them or that there will be a union of sperm and ovum. Giving birth is viewed as inevitable and desirable. On the other hand, the young boy of 6 is small relative to the general population. He is hairless, has a high-pitched voice, and is small in stature. Other than the penis, the boy does not have the male attributes that he wants and expects to have. Striving to be strong, large, powerful, and dominant, traits that define the male gender, young male children are likely to select toys, games, roles, and activities that reflect such attributes. Ullian (1981) suggests that this developmental discontinuity in male sex-role functioning leads to excessive competition, aggression, and anger. It may be an exaggerated response to the developmental task of establishing a clear male identity (Ullian 1981).

Biological reductionists invoke science as objective knowledge that is free from political or social bias. For instance, Brigham (1923) argued that immigration from Eastern and Southern Europe be restricted because people from that area score low on intelligence tests. However, Brigham stated that this process should be done to preserve the current intelligence level in America and should be dictated by science and not socio-political factors. However, it is clear that the eugenics movement influenced this decision. Even Cyril Burt, working through the nonexistent Ms. Conway (1959), attempted to show that IQ is based on genetics instead of social ideals. Bias against immigrants and blacks has always played a role in scientific endeavors. Contrary to statements by both Brigham and Burt, their motivation is questionable (or known).

All individuals are biased because of the environment in which they are enculturated and scientifically socialized. However, scientists believe they are objective because they follow prescribed codes of science. However, no scientist and therefore no scientific endeavor is completely objective. All are subject to preconceived notions of what they believe ought to be true rather than what is true. Hypotheses are generated with a social and a cultural bias to the process. This bias cannot be divorced from the "scientific process" that one learns as a member of the "scientific community." While everyone should have the opportunity to participate in scientific endeavors, we should all be aware of the socialization process behind the scientific inquiry.

REFERENCES

Allport, G.W. 1954. *The Nature of Prejudice*. Reading, Mass.: Addison-Wesley.
Alper, J.S. 1977. Biological Determinism. *Telos* 31:1 64–172.
Bacon, F. 1955. *Selected Writings of Francis Bacon*. New York: Modern Library.
Baker, P.T. 1958. The Biological Adaptation of Man to Hot Deserts. *American Naturalist* 92: 237–257.
———. 1977. Ecological and Physiological Adaptations in Indigenous South Americans. In P.T. Baker and J.S. Weiner, eds., *The Biology of Human Adaptability*. Oxford: Clarendon Press.
Brigham, C.C. 1923. *A Study of American Intelligence*. Princeton, N.J.: Princeton University Press.
Brown, D. 1957. Masculinity Femininity Development in Children. *Journal of Consultant Psychology* 27: 197–205.
Caplan, A.L. 1984. Sociobiology as a Strategy in Science. *The Monist* 67: 143–160.
Caplan, N. and Nelson, S. 1973. On Being Useful. The Nature and Consequences of Psychological Research on Social Problems. *American Psychologist* 3: 199–211.
Conway, J. 1959. Class Differences in General Intelligence: II. *British Journal of Statistical Psychology* 12: 5–14.
Coon, C.S. 1982. *Racial Adaptations*. Chicago: Nelson-Hall.
Davies, J. 1955. *Phrenology, Fad and Science*. New Haven, Conn.: Yale University Press.
Eisenberg, J.F. 1981. *The Mammalian Radiations: An Analysis of Trends in Evolution, Adaptation, and Behavior*. Chicago: University of Chicago Press.
Erickson, P.A. 1979. Phrenology and Physical Anthropology: The George Combe Connection. *Occasional Papers in Anthropology*. No. 6, Nova Scotia, Canada: Saint Mary's University.
Fuller, S. 1987. On Regulating What is Known: A Way to Social Epistemology. *Synthese* 73: 145–183.
Gabor, T. and Roberts, J.V. 1990. Rushton on Race and Crime: The Evidence Remains Unconvincing. *Canadian Journal of Criminology*. April, 335–343.
Goodman, M. 1952. *Race Awareness in Young Children*. Cambridge, Mass.: Addison-Wesley.
Gossett, T.F. 1965. *Race: The History of an Idea in America*. New York: Schocken Books.
Gould, S.J. 1977. *Ever Since Darwin*. New York: W.W. Norton.
———. 1980. Sociobiology and the Theory of Natural Selection. In G.W. Barlow and J. Silverberg, eds., *Sociobiology: Beyond Nature/Nurture?* Boulder, Colo.: Westview Press, pp. 257–269.
———. 1981. *The Mismeasure of Man*. New York: W.W. Norton.
Gould, S.J. and Lewontin, R.C. 1979. The Spandrels of San Marco and the Panglossian Paradigm: A Critique of the Adaptationist Programme. *Proceedings of the Royal Society of London* B205: 581–598.

Harpending, H., Rogers, A. and Draper, P. 1987. Human Sociobiology. *Yearbook of Physical Anthropology* 30: 127-150.
Hartley, R. 1959. Sex-Role Pressures and the Socialization of the Male Child. *Psychological Research* 5: 457-468.
Howells, W.W. 1973. *Cranial Variation in Man*. Peabody Museum Papers, Vol. 67, Cambridge, Mass.: Harvard University Press.
Irons, W. 1981. Sociobiology and Levels of Explanation. *American Anthropologist* 83: 147-149.
Jensen, A.R. 1969. How Much Can We Boost IQ and Scholastic Achievement? *Harvard Educational Review* 39: 1-129.
———. 1972. *Genetics and Education*. New York: Harper and Row.
Kagan, J. 1956. The Child's Perception of the Parent. *Journal of Abnormal Social Psychology* 53: 257–258.
Katz, P.A. 1973. Perception of Racial Cues in Preschool Children: A New Look. *Developmental Psychology* 8(2): 295-299.
———. 1976. The Acquisition of Racial Attitudes in Children. In P.A. Katz ed., *Towards the Elimination of Racism*. New York: Pergamon Press Inc.
Katz, P.A. and Zalk, S.R. 1974. Doll Preferences: An Index of Racial Attitudes? *Journal of Educational Psychology* 66(5): 663–668.
Katz, P.A., Sohn, M., and Zalk, S.R. 1975. Perceptual Concomitants of Racial Attitudes in Urban Grade School Children. *Developmental Psychology* 11(2): 135–144.
Kohlberg, L. A. 1966. Cognitive Developmental Analysis of Children's Sex-Role Concepts and Attitudes. In R. Friedman, R. Richart and R. Vande Wiele, eds., *Sex Differences in Behavior*. New York: John Wiley.
Kuhn, T.S. 1962. *The Structure of Scientific Revolutions*. Chicago: University of Chicago Press.
Laudan, L. 1977. *Progress and Its Problems: Toward a Theory of Scientific Growth*. Los Angeles: University of California Press.
Livingstone, F.B. 1958. Anthropological Implications of Sickle Cell Gene Distribution in West Africa. *American Anthropologist* 60: 533–562.
Lovejoy, C.O. 1981. The Origin of Man. *Science* 211: 341–350.
Lynn, D. 1962. Sex-role and Parental Identification. *Child Development* 33: 555–564.
Mannheim, K. 1940. *Man and Society in an Age of Reconstruction*. London: Routledge and Kegan Paul.
McCoy, R.W. 1985. Phrenology and Popular Gullibility. *The Skeptical Inquirer* 9: 261-268.
McLaren, A. 1981. A Prehistory of the Social Sciences: Phrenology in France. *Comparative Study of Society and History* 21: 3–22.
Mead, M. 1928. *Coming of Age in Samoa*. New York: William Morrow.
Milic, V. 1984. Sociology of Knowledge and Sociology of Science. *Social Science Information* 23(2): 213–274.
Millett, K. 1971. *Sexual Politics*. London: Rupert Hart-Davis.
Morton, S.G. 1839. *Crania Americana*. Philadelphia: John Pennington.
Nassi, J.A. and Abramowitz, S.I. 1976. From Phrenology to Psychosurgery and Back Again: Biological Studies of Criminality. *American Journal Orthopsychiatric* 46(4): 591–607.
Proshansky, H. 1966. The Development of Intergroup Attitudes. In I.W. Hoffman and M.L. Hoffman, eds., *Review of Child Development Research*, Vol. 2. New York: Russell Sage Foundation.

Rose, S. 1979. It's Only Human Nature: The Sociobiologist's Fairyland. *Race and Class* 20(3): 277–287.

Rushton, J.P. 1985. Differential K Theory: The Sociobiology of Individual and Group Differences. *Personality and Individual Differences* 6(4): 441–452.

———. 1988a. Race Differences in Behavior: A Review and Evolutionary Analysis. *Personality and Individual Differences* 9(6): 1009–1024.

———. 1988b. The Reality of Racial Differences: A Rejoinder with New Evidence. Personality and Individual Differences 9(6): 1035–1040.

Stepan, N. 1982. *The Idea of Race in Science: Great Britain 1800–1960*. United Kingdom: Macmillan Press, Ltd.

Tiger, L. 1969. *Men in Groups*. London: Nelson.

———. 1971. The Possible Biological Origins of Sexual Discrimination. *Impact of Science on Society* 20: 29–44.

Ullian, D.Z. 1981. Why Boys Will Be Boys: A Structural Perspective. *American Journal of Orthopsychiatry* 51: 493–501.

Washburn, S.L. 1978. Animal Behavior and Social Anthropology. *Society* 15(6): 35–41.

Williams, J.E. 1966. Connotations of Racial Concepts and Color Names. *Journal of Personality and Social Psychology* 3(5): 531–540.

Williams, J.E. and Morland, J.K. 1976. *Race, Color, and the Young Child*. Chapel Hill, N.C.: University of North Carolina Press.

Williams, J.E., Tucker, R.D., and Dunham, F.Y. 1971. Changes in the Connotations of Color Names Among Negroes and Caucasians: 1963–1969. *Journal of Personality and Social Psychology* 19(2): 222–228.

Wilson, E.O. 1975a. *Sociobiology: The New Synthesis*. Cambridge, Mass.: Harvard University Press.

———. 1975b. Human Decency is an Animal. *New York Times Magazine* 12 (October): 38–48.

Wolpoff, M. 1985. Human Evolution at the Peripheries: The Pattern at the Eastern Edge. In Phillip V. Tobias, ed., *Hominid Evolution: Past, Present and Future*, Proceedings of the Taung Diamond Jubilee International Symposium, Johannesburg and Mmabatho, Southern Africa. New York: Alan R. Liss Publishers, pp. 355–365.

CHAPTER 3

Tarzan in the Classroom: How "Educational" Films Mythologize Africa and Miseducate Americans

Sheila S. Walker with Jennifer Rasamimanana

Both commercial and educational media images of Africa and Afro-America, in the large sense, continue to portray inaccurate and derogatory images of people of Africa and of African descent. Such images, in addition to misinforming viewers, perpetuates divisive and destructive negative stereotyping which affects both African Americans and non-African Americans. The nature of such images and their effects are described and analyzed.

MYTHS AND MISCONCEPTIONS: THE MISREPRESENTATION OF AFRICA

How do you react to the term "Africa?" What is the first word that comes to mind? Don't take time to think. Just React. Emotionally. "Dark continent," "savages," "lion," "jungle," "Tarzan," "primitive," "mysterious," "spear?" Any others? Surely the second largest continental land mass on the face of the earth must have a few other characteristics. As a continent, like Europe and Asia, it must have some diversity. What are [Africans'] nationalities? How many languages do they speak? What religions do they practice? What are their historical and cultural achievements? (Maynard 1974: v)

In 1979 the African Studies Center at Michigan State University organized a conference on "Images of Africa: New Directions in Media." The tone of the conference presenters was one of scholarly outrage at the fact that not only commercial, but also "educational" media portrayed the kinds of inaccurate and denigrating images of Africa that made the opening quote both evocative and provocative. These educators and analysts of educational media were uniformly critical of the available materials, which, they agreed, presented overwhelmingly inaccurate, unrepresentative, stereotyped, and demeaning views of African life. To date, the situation has changed little. Few new directions have been taken, and the same impressions of Africa prevail. A 1990 Rockefeller Foundation report, *A Greater Voice for Africa in the Schools*, based on the findings of a group formed to discuss changes in teaching about Africa since the publication of a 1967 Carnegie Corporation report *(Informing Americans About Africa)*, drew the lamentable conclusion that, as in 1967, Africa remains the most neglected world area in the school curriculum (Jacqz 1967; Rich, Renyi, and Friedrich 1990). Both reports identify contemporary media representations of Africa and Africans as major contributors to this situation.

Discussing the problem at the 1979 conference, African-American educator Evelyn Jones Rich, who also chaired the 1990 Rockefeller group, noted the following:

Twenty years after Africa was recognized as a serious educational topic, hundreds of films, film strips, tape cassettes, records and audio tapes later, there are at most two dozen examples of audio-visual materials—electronic and print—which present a realistic image of Africa and its people. Yet, the results most often reinforced, negative images of Africa which focus on the sensational, laud the modern to the disadvantage of the traditional, and underline the idea that western culture is both desirable and superior. (Rich 1979: 1)

The Rockefeller Report noted that new scholarship about Africa has not yet permeated school curricula and discussed the larger implications of the continued miseducation about Africa for the education of all Americans:

Myths and misapprehensions, distortions, sheer neglect, and covert racism . . . continue to prevail in our schools. These issues particularly plague the study of Africa, a continent of diverse and dynamic peoples, many of whose descendants have been major forces in the growth and definition of our own democracy and in the African diaspora throughout the world. The study of Africa and Africans has special meaning and importance as we go about the task of learning not only how to live as global citizens but also how to define ourselves—all of us, black, white, Asian, Native American and others—as citizens of our own democracy. (Rich 1990: 4–5)

Anthropologist Paul Bohannon (1974) asserts that "only if the myth is stripped away can the reality of Africa emerge" (Bohannon 1974:1). Concerning the myth that Africa was "savage," Bohannon concludes that "*savages became a philosophical necessity for the emergence of Europe*" [italics added]. Savages, both depraved and noble, explained historical as well as psychic problems—but the ideas concerning savages were buttressed with few facts" (Bohannon 1974:4). He cites a text widely used in high schools (Roehm and Buskem's *Records of Mankind*, published in 1970), which states categorically that "most of the Negroes in Africa may be classified as barbarians," and argues that "teaching and learning about Africa takes place against a background which views the continent and its people as inferior and underdeveloped" (Bohannon 1974:9). As a result of "inadequate and distorted curricula [that] tend to focus on the exotic, the sensational, and the negative [m]ost white (and many black) Americans continue to feel superior to Africans and people of African descent and consequently do not see the validity of the worldviews of the indigenous people of Africa" (Bohannon 1974:9).

As Europeans first enslaved Africans to work the plantations of the Americas, and subsequently conquered and colonized African peoples on their home continent, they developed complex justifications for their actions: "In order to rationalize their brutal exploitation, the Europeans began to develop pseudoscientific explanations for their innate superiority over conquered Black Africans. Thus, in the sixteenth, seventeenth, and eighteenth centuries, a detailed philosophy of racism was written to justify the conquest of Africa" (Maynard 1974: 13).

Discussing the evolution of the myth of the "dark continent" and the details of its perpetuation by both the American and European film industries, Maynard cites the Tarzan legend created by American writer Edgar Rice Burroughs (1875–1950) as the best-known example of this tradition of distortion. Although Burroughs never set foot in Africa, his books, and the films based on them, have constituted the major source of misinformation on Africa for many generations.[1]

Myths about Africa were thus created, popularized, and perpetuated through both racist scholarship and racist popular literature. In the 20th century, however, they have been most efficiently propagated through motion pictures. As African-American critic Lindsay Patterson (1974), in discussing Hollywood films using Africa as a locale, noted in the mid-1970s: "Despite the political, social, and economic changes occurring [in Africa] within the last two decades, the films persisted in presenting Africa as the lost, dark continent, populated by stupid, bloodthirsty savages" (Patterson 1974:78). Commenting at the Images of Africa conference on films on Africa from major educational media distributors such as Encyclopedia Britannica Films, McGraw-Hill Films and Filmstrips, and the National Geographic Society for Current Affairs, Marylee Wiley (1979) concluded the following:

African societies are typified as backward and static. The implicit assumption . . . is the superiority of the cultures of the industrialized people. There is no evidence that we have much to learn from African peoples. We may learn about them but they advance only by learning from us. This is a very dangerous attitude to develop in students who will be leaders in this society in the coming years. (Wiley 1979:7)

Another conference presenter, Joseph Adjaye (1979), noted that the media on Africa tend to overgeneralizations such as "Africans live in villages," which fully ignore those millions of Africans who live in urban areas. According to Adjaye, another common generalization is that "Africa is hot and humid"; in fact, many areas of the continent are cool and/or dry.[2] Other clear misrepresentations cited by Adjaye, such as "Africa is a country," abound in the U.S. public's assumptions. This particular misperception is especially striking given that Africa is more than three times the size of the United States, and is composed of more than 50 countries and over a thousand distinct ethnic cultures. The media also manifest a fascination with issues they can portray as sensational and bizarre, often presenting Africa as a land of barbarous natives whose major pastime is to dance half-naked to drum music (Adjaye 1979).

Maynard's examination exposes larger questions: Why do whites feel the need to portray distorted versions of African realities? Why do the Western media continue to perpetuate myths about Africa, in updated versions, when accurate realities could be portrayed instead? Why is the general public, particularly schoolchildren, still consistently and systematically misinformed about Africa? Why, in view of the amount of accurate information currently available, do filmmakers continue to create, and others continue to distribute, show, and view such inaccurate portrayals of Africa as both commercial entertainment and educational tools? Maynard provides an answer to this fundamental question: "The implications of this misconception reflect the fundamental crisis in American race relations. As long as this erroneous concept lingers, dominant white attitudes toward African Americans as inferiors can be rationalized. How can any race of people whose ancestors were spear-toting savages be considered equal?" (Maynard 1974:vi)

U.S. PUBLIC SCHOOL IMAGES OF PEOPLES OF AFRICAN ANCESTRY: CASE STUDY OF A "MODEL" SCHOOL DISTRICT

In 1980 I undertook an analysis of the collection of educational films on Africa in a major urban public school district with a multi-ethnic, predominantly African-American population. My goal was to test the findings of the Images of Africa conference in a state (California) and school district that prided themselves on their sensitivity to issues of ethnic pluralism and cultural diversity. Because the school district is located in a cosmopolitan area in close proximity to major universities with Africanist faculty, students, and others with accurate knowledge of Africa as well as extensive library resources on Africa, I anticipated that the district's film collection on Africa would reflect a relatively higher level of accuracy than would those in school districts with fewer easily accessible resources and less awareness of and stated appreciation for cultural diversity. To establish the representivness of the model district's films, I compared its film holdings, most of which were from major distributors, with those of several school districts across the country. I requested that a public school teacher and a university professor knowledgeable about Africa and the African Diaspora also view the films, and I compared their independent critiques with my own.

Due to the obvious relationship between the portrayal of Africa and the portrayals of all people of African ancestry (a relationship also noted by Bohannon, Maynard, and others), I enlarged the initial focus of my study beyond the African continent to examine film images of Africa's human and cultural extensions in the Americas. Thus, after viewing the majority of the films on Africa in the model district's film library to get a sense of the nature of the images of Africa they presented, I sought to ascertain the relationship between these images of Africa to media images of peoples of the African Diaspora in the Americas. I also viewed most of the district's holdings of films on African Americans in the United States and all of its very few films on the Caribbean and those areas of South America with significant populations of African ancestry (see Table 3.1). The images presented by the model district's films proved comparable to both those of the other school districts and those already identified by previous researchers.

Table 3.1
"Educational" Film Holdings on Africa and People of African Ancestry in a Model Public School District's Film Library and Viewed for This Study

Films on Africa
  Africa Is My Home
  African Girl—Malobi
  Black and White in South Africa
  Continent of Africa: Lands Below the Sahara
  Dr. Leakey and the Dawn of Man
  East Africa: The Multi-Racial Experience
  East Africa: Two Life Styles
  Imani: Beegie and the Egg
  New Africa: People and Leaders
  Nigeria: A School for Jacob
  Nigeria: Africa in Miniature
  The Nile Valley and Its People
  Of Times, Tombs, and Treasures: The Treasures of Tutankhamon
  Ujima: Modupe and the Flood
  West Africa: Two Life Styles
  Zambia
On the Caribbean
  Jamaica
  Kuumba
  The West Indies
On South America
  Brazil: People of the Highlands
  Brazil: The Vanishing Negro
  Colombia and Venezuela
  Flavio
  South America
  South America: Life in the City
On the United States
  The Color of Man

Table 3.1 cont.

Heritage of the Negro
Umoja:The Tiger and the Big Wind
We Came to America
What Color Are You?

Film Critique, Analysis, and Comparison

I drew several conclusions after viewing the films, most of which were corroborated by the independent critiques of the collaborating public school teacher and university professor. First, despite the numerous available published works providing detailed critiques of the film images of Africans and peoples of African ancestry, and despite the abundance of local experts and library resources, the model public school district's visual resources on Africa and the African Diaspora were, with very few notable exceptions, inaccurate, misleading, and pejorative. Almost all of the films on Africa exhibited the worst imaginable and well-documented stereotypes. This finding also held true for the film holdings of other school districts that were compared. Second, these film holdings best reflected the magnitude of Euro-American misconceptions and misrepresentations about Africa, Africans, and, by extension, people of African ancestry. Third, overgeneralization was (and continues to be) a major problem common to films on Africa.

European colonization and its sequels are presented as unmitigatedly positive because they resulted in Africans giving up their "primitive" lifestyles. Mention is not made of how many Africans fought determinedly against European aggression and influence to preserve their indigenous and sovereign ways. None of the films note that many contemporary, well-educated, and cosmopolitan Africans have chosen to maintain their indigenous values and behaviors, or that many others have eclectically adapted or "Africanized" some elements of Western culture while deliberately and consciously rejecting others as inferior to their own. It is also striking that the films viewed consistently represent whites in a positive light for what they have done for and given to Africa, not what they have done to and continue to do to Africa or get from Africa. Films such as *Nigeria: A School for Jacob* and *New Africa: Peoples and Leaders* exemplify this approach in that they present no discussion of the systematic impoverishment of Africa first by the transatlantic slave trade and then by European colonialism. European and American direct and indirect political and economic support of the racist regime in South Africa is also conveniently ignored.

In most of the films viewed, life in Africa, with the exception of that of the Westernized sectors—should they be acknowledged to exist—is presented as materially difficult. Generally, what could be viewed by a U.S. audience as positive aspects of indigenous African life are either not mentioned or are portrayed in a negative light. Traditional lifestyles are negatively contrasted with the recently acquired Westernized lifestyles of a small minority of Africans. In *Africa Is My Home*, for example, the traditional lifestyle is characterized as "the bondage of the past," and is explicitly contrasted with "dreams of tomorrow."

Language usage is an important issue in the continuing miseducation of Americans about Africa via "educational" films. The language of most of the films is overloaded with words that, when used in other contexts, may be innocent and devoid of value judgments. When used to describe Africa and Africans, however, they invariably carry prejudicial undertones and invidious connotations. A prime example is the term *native*, meaning simply someone originally from a particular place, but it has acquired a derogatory connotation when applied to Africans. It suggests stupidity and inherent inferiority by evoking images of bands of scantily clad spear throwers who are consistently outwitted in their own environment by whites (a la Tarzan). This pejorative, cinematically created image of African "natives," in addition to being difficult, if not impossible, to find in contemporary Africa, was not balanced in any of the films by current images of fashionably suited or traditionally dressed business or sophisticated professional women "natives" of Africa who live and work in the continent's cosmopolitan cities. It does not spare even heads of state, diplomats, wealthy businesspeople, or scholars, thus linking them inextricably and inappropriately with the invidious image the word evokes in the European or American mind. Both *Zambia* and *Nigeria: Africa in Miniature* begin with stereotypical images of African "natives" dancing to drums. In *Africa Is My Home*, the "natives'" daily activities are accompanied by drum rhythms—as if Africans played drums all day!

Zambia, which the model district just acquired before I undertook this analysis, was praised by an administrator with whom I had discussed my dismay at the nature of the films I had viewed. However, I found this film to be as conceptually distressing as most of the others, although its slicker technique served to somewhat obscure its flagrant problems for at least some viewers. For example, the film's cameraperson seemed obsessed with the bare feet of some of the rural Zambians in the film as if to say, visually, "see how primitive they are." They focus on the sleeping conditions in the house of the large Zambian family that is the subject of the film and the frequent, lingering close-ups of the sole one-eyed son firmly reinforce the idea that life in Africa is awful. Obviously, almost all Africans have two eyes, and many Africans have their own beds to the extent that they value individualistic values rather than the kind of communal values that would make sharing a bed with siblings both normal and desirable. Obviously, such visual images had been deliberately selected out of an infinity of possibilities. They seem to have been specifically chosen to convey a negative message rather than to explain the meanings that are the basis of understanding a different lifestyle.

The West Indies presented a superficial and confusing view of this very varied group of islands, and conveyed the clear message that life is miserable here if you're not a white tourist. Two films on South America, *Colombia and*

Venezuela, and *South America*, were both poor quality, dated films that essentially ignored the presence of the significant populations of African ancestry in both countries. When shown in *South America: Life in the Cities*, people of African ancestry were portrayed exclusively and explicitly as examples of the poor of Rio de Janeiro, Brazil, with no reference to their presence in all the other nations of South America. This emphasis on poverty as if it were the only reality of people of African ancestry in Brazil fails to address the obvious cultural role that Afro-Brazilians play in their nation. Similarly, the dated film, *Brazil: People of the Highlands*, which claims that some Brazilians have only "traces" of African (or Indian) ancestry, obscures the acknowledged fact that the African contribu-tion is the very basis of Brazilian popular culture. Although Brazil has the world's second largest population of people of African origin after Nigeria, the only specific commentary on the more than 50 million Afro-Brazilians is found in the film with the marvelously provocative title, *Brazil: The Vanishing Negro*, which examines that nation's racial problems, particularly the Brazilian social policy of "whitening." In the hands of a knowledgeable teacher, the film could provide a wonderful tool for exploring Brazil's myth of racial democracy. Presented uncritically, it can only serve to convey a confusing message about Brazil's color-coded social relationship.

The sterotypical and often seemingly contrived visual imagery in many of the films viewed reinforces Eurocentric misperceptions about Africa and its people. The nude adults shown in *The Nile Valley and Its People*, for example, are guaranteed to shock U.S. schoolchildren and assure them that Africans are indeed "primitive." The filmmaker's selection of such an image serves to portray the exact antithesis of the African norm and ignores the reality that the overwhelming majority of Africans wear clothes that cover much more of their bodies than do Westerners. Indeed, many Africans' first exposure to public near-nudity is on those African beaches where sun-seeking white female tourists flock to go topless, often seriously offending African morality.

The problem of overgeneralization is most evident in films such as *New Africa: People and Leaders* and *Continent of Africa*. Such films are disjointed and confusing, presenting superficial smatterings of information from different parts of Africa without giving viewers a sense of the geopolitical setting of the people or phenomena on which they focus. Africa is treated as an undifferentiated unit, as a country rather than a continent of extremely varied cultures and terrains. Such overgeneralization is tantamount to visiting only New York City and formulating an impression of the United States. This approach is especially reprehensible and misleading given that Africa is the most culturally diverse of the world's continents.

Although some of the films on Africa allude to important issues regarding aspects of African life such as polygamy, the problems of monoculture cash crop economies, the effects of Western education, and even the myths of the "dark continent," these issues tend to be merely mentioned, not examined or explained. Discussion of these issues could be used as a basis for understanding; but when presented alone, without clarification, they only contribute to the depiction of Africa as irrational, illogical, and problem-ridden.

The most egregiously offensive film in the collection, *Black and White in South Africa*, represents what even the most uncritical viewer should recognize as a flagrant example of ethnocentric fimmaking. It begins by saying, "When the Dutch arrived at the Cape of Good Hope, they found no one there but some dark-skinned nomads." The film then goes on to present a history of that nation from a perspective that is unabashedly sympathetic to white South Africans, failing to mention, even in passing, the White minority's extreme oppression of the African majority. The rosy picture presented of South African society in this film contrasts starkly with the negative images of other African societies presented in most of the films in the model district's collection. There is a lesson to be learned here of the perspective on Africa and people of African ancestry it conveys. That this situation may have developed inadvertently due to ignorance or inattention rather than deliberately is irrelevant. The educational results, and the larger ramifications thereof, are inescapable.

That this film was part of the district's collection indicated that school personnel had specifically selected it from among other possibilities and that it was available for use by educators for the express purpose of teaching children about life in Africa. One school administrator took umbrage at my objection to finding such a film in the collection, saying that teachers knew such films were inaccurate and therefore did not use them. However, when I later wanted to use the film in a workshop with teachers concerning the problem, it was unavailable because a teacher was using it in a class!

I would like to have believed that the teacher in question was using the film critically to raise student consciousness concerning media manipulations of reality, for which it would have been ideal. Unfortunatey, my interactions with teachers from that school suggested that such optimism would have been inappropriate. On the contrary, these teachers were products of the worldview (and the educational system on which it is based) that allowed such images to be present in the educational institution in the first place. Those who attended the workshop found nothing wrong with the films I showed them from their own school collection until the stereotypes, distortions, and misrepresentations were pointed out and explained.

That such a visual portrayal of South Africa should be found in a U.S. public school film collection without the balance of even one of the numerous existing film representations of the African majority perspective on South Africa is an outrage unless the educational goal is to perpetuate among our nation's children an appreciation for the world's most blatant modern form of racial oppression. A perfect use of such a film would be to show it in conjunction with films reflecting the black South African perspective. Such an exercise would help to teach students about the manipulation of reality in film and about the ways in which image makers can represent and misrepresent human frailties. Such a lesson would prepare them to be critical viewers and equip them with a means for what Noam Chomsky calls "intellectual self-defense"—that is, a critical attitude toward the media that create so much of the public's worldview (Szykowny 1990).

Exemplary Exceptions

The notable exceptions to what was otherwise a dismal rule regarding images of Africa and the African Diaspora are the very films in which the subjects are allowed to speak about their own lives. *Jamaica*, one of the best of the films viewed, presents the island from such a balanced, insider's perspective. *Kuumba* (Kiswahili for "creativity"), an animated film created by the African-American-owned Nguzo Saba Productions to teach children the "Seven Principles of Blackness," effectively uses the Trinidadian steel drum as its example. The three other Nguzo Saba films in the model district's film collection—*Imani* ("faith"): *Beegie and the Egg; Ujima* ("collective work and responsibility"): *Modupe and the Flood*, and *Umoja* ("unity"): *The Tiger and the Big Wind*—illustrate others of the Seven Principles with examples from Africa and Afro-America. They provide refreshing highlights in the otherwise distressingly miseducational collection. The availability in the collection of such accurate, informative, and uplifting films proves that the collection need not have been as bad as it was. Obviously, several good films were available for purchase at the time of the study. This availability makes even less understandable the continued acquisition and use of clearly offensive films.

THEORY VERSUS REALITY IN THE U.S. PUBLIC SCHOOL WORLDVIEW

The 1980 *History/Social Science Framework for Public Schools*, published by the California State Department of Education Office of Public Instruction (1981), proclaims that students should have "respect for the dignity of all human beings, regardless of race, sex, religion, or belief" and should acquire "an in-depth understanding of the diversity and commonality of human experience as manifest in the history and culture of the many racial, ethnic, and social groups which form our society and which comprise the global community" (1981:5). According to the *Framework,* students should learn about "both the similarities and differences among individuals and societies," the "human needs and life experiences common to all peoples," "why human societies develop different 'ways of life' or diverse cultures," and the "reasons for variations in human appearances and behaviors" of the world's diverse peoples. They should learn, in addition to material facts, how different groups of people "see themselves and how others see them." The *Framework* also states that "human values are not based on a single standard, but are inherently diverse from time to time and from place to place and from group to group," and "no single belief system should be imposed upon students or held up to ridicule."

Of particular relevance is the *Framework*'s contention that students should be taught to evaluate information presented in books, periodicals, and other media in order to *"detect ethnocentricity, and/or other biases in presentation* [italics added]" (1981:6). Under "Education Code Requirements Affecting History and Social Science Instruction," the *Framework* offers several specifications regarding the educational materials to be used in the schools, including:

Portrayal of Cultural and Racial Diversity:
60040. When adopting materials for use in the schools, governing boards shall include only instructional materials which, in their determination, accurately portray the cultural and racial diversity of our society.
Prohibited Instructional Materials
60044. No instructional materials shall be adopted by any governing
board for use in the schools which, in its determination, contain:
(a) Any matter reflecting adversely upon persons because of their race,
color, creed, national origin, ancestry, sex, or occupation. (1981:40–41)

The *Framework* emphasizes that "all textbooks and related instructional materials in history/social science should be accurate, objective, current, and suited to the needs and comprehension of pupils at respective grade levels"(1981:41). Moreover, "the major criteria" for evaluating such materials "should reflect a philosophy consistent with that of the *History/Social Science Framework*" (1981:37).

The specifications and caveats of this document are indeed noble and laudable. Not surprisingly, the 1988 revised version of the *Framework* reiterates such positive educational goals in somewhat different language. From the foregoing film critique and discussion, however, it is apparent that almost all of the films on Africa and the African Diaspora found in the model school district's film library in 1980 were in direct contravention of both the philosophy and the specific provisions of the *Framework*. Rather than teaching students to "esteem others' individual and group heritages" and have "respect for the dignity of all human beings," these films teach students to depreciate and disdain the peoples and lifestyles of Africa and, by extension, people of African ancestry, by presenting them as inferior and often quite strange. Rather than fostering "an in-depth understanding of the diversity and commonality of human experience," these films, which are presented to U.S. schoolchildren as part of their compulsory education, teach inaccurate, negative myths about the Africans who are the ancestors of the African-American population of the United States. Nonetheless, their presence in this California school district's film library implies that they satisfy, as per Specification 60045, the governing board's criteria for accuracy, objectivity, and currency!

In violation of the provision concerning prohibited instructional materials, the district's film holdings present images and messages that consistently denigrate the African ancestry and heritage of African Americans and other people of African descent in the Americas. In violation of the provision that instructional materials be "accurate, objective, and current," most of the materials on Africa and the African Diaspora contain inexcusable inaccuracies. While many of the films are of poor quality and limited value because they are old, there is no justification for purchasing newer films like *Zambia*. Although these new films employ sophisticated media techniques that prevent uncritical viewers from perceiving these problems, they manifest the same kinds of inaccuracies, stereotypes, and Eurocentric insults to peoples of Africa as do the earlier acquisitions.

The question that obviously arises then is Why retain the majority of these films on Africa and the African Diaspora if they are in clear violation of the specific provisions of the Office of Public Instruction of the California State Department of Education? These films violate both the overall philosophy and the specific criteria of the 1980 *Framework*, and thus they should have been removed—*unless the worldview they portray is the one the state's governing board deliberately chose to convey and even impose on its students.*

In 1991, I reexamined the educational film holdings of the model and other selected school districts. This follow-up study revealed no significant changes in the districts' film holdings, a finding that supports the conclusions of the 1990 Rockefeller report. Those who have become more informed about Africa in the present period, and they represent but a minute segment of the U.S. population, have informed themselves in spite of, rather than as a result of, the nation's educational system and its instructional materials.

RAMIFICATIONS OF MISREPRESENTING AND MYTHOLOGIZING AFRICA AND THE AFRICAN DIASPORA

The vision of any lifestyle a filmmaker chooses to portray is determined quite arbitrarily based on the filmmakers' own interests, perspectives, and biases rather than on any kind of objective reality. Thus, very different visions and versions can be created depending on the ideological criteria a filmmaker selects. Judging from the content of the "educational" films viewed, the selected criteria apparently decree that peoples of Africa and of African ancestry should be portrayed in an unfavorable light. Given the vision and perspectives of the films viewed as examples of representative teaching aids, it is easy to understand the stereotyped statements that both adults and children who have been educated in the U.S. school system often make about Africa and Africans. Children of all backgrounds have been and continue to be inculcated with negative opinions and misconceptions about peoples of Africa and thus, by extension, people of African ancestry.

In view of the images consistently presented in such "educational" films, what chance do African-American children have of acquiring even a neutral, as opposed to a clearly negative, impression of their own ethnic heritage and, hence, of themselves and their role in both U.S. and global society? African Americans have been deeply affected by the steady barrage of negative images of Africa and people of African descent propagated by both the commercial and educational media. According to Nigerian scholar Oladipo Onipede:

> The effect of Hollywood's holy war against Africa is most pronounced on the average American black man. Like the rest of the public, he is an American, and most of his information on Africa comes from the mass media available to him. Furthermore, because the American black man constitutes a minority—a persecuted one indeed—his immediate reaction is to divest himself of any traits associated with the symbol of the "savage African." (1974:72)

Many contemporary problems of the African-American community have been well-documented. Poverty, unemployment, drug addiction, illiteracy, and a high rate of teenage pregnancy have been identified as influential factors in the deteriorating values and lifestyles of an important segment of the African-American community. Experts have suggested many reasons for the development of these problems and have posed an even greater number of solutions. There is one factor, however, that is identified consistently as being both the most devastating and the most easily correctable source of many of these problems: the absence of a positive self-image is directly linked to the underachievement of many young African Americans. According to Rashid (1984): "For African American children a sense of pride and identification with one's ethnic roots is a vital prerequisite for coping with the racism and classism that permeate this society. When young African American children feel positive about themselves and their ethnic heritage, positive feelings about school and community are the next logical steps" (1984:13–14).

Awareness of this issue, and of the relationship between perceptions of Africa and the behavior of African Americans, is by no means recent. As early as 1933, African-American historian Carter G. Woodson argued that Euro-American society, and especially its system of compulsory education, presented distorted perspectives on African history and culture so that African Americans would be induced to deny and negate their ancestral heritage. Indeed, African Americans have been alternately taught that they either have no heritage or that their ancestors were primitive tree-dwellers who had no culture. According to Warren Robbins, formerly of the Frederick Douglass Institute of Negro Arts and History in Washington, D.C.: "The wide-spread myth that the Negro American has no past other than slavery and savagery has constituted one of the most tragic—and unnecessary—stumbling blocks to his thinking about himself" (cited in Anosinke 1982:438). Hilliard (1978) provides a logical and well-documented explanation for why consistently inaccurate, negative, and denigrating images of Africa were created in the first place, and why they continue to be so assiduously and systematically perpetuated despite the availability of accurate information that clearly contradicts them. Associating media images of Africa with the images and treatment of African Americans in the United States, Hilliard maintains that the fundamental issue is the Euro-

American creation and maintenance of a racial and cultural image that justifies the continued exploitation of Africans and oppression of African Americans:

> The history and culture of colonized or dominated people is usually destroyed or distorted. This enables an oppressor to hold a view of the oppressed which will justify self-serving interventions by the oppressor. It also serves the function of confusing the oppressed group regarding its own identity and resources, thus limiting its ability to respond to oppression. The worldview and cultural information of the oppressed group is manipulated, and truth becomes a scarce commodity. (Hilliard 1978:110)

Hilliard concludes, like Woodson did more than half a century earlier, that "by the control and production of information, the control of a people's belief and behavior will follow" (1978:112).

How then does the systematic inculcation of such negative images of peoples of Africa and their descendants in the Americas, including the United States, influence the attitudes of whites toward them? Such derogatory misconceptions foster attitudes of entrenched ethnocentrism on the part of Euro-American students and thus help widen the already large gap in understanding between Euro-Americans and African Americans. Patterson (1974) notes that the message Hollywood films give to the world is the Euro-American doctrine that "to be white is an infinitely more desirable human state than any other" (Patterson 1974:76). This "white is best" message comes through so loudly and with such persistent clarity in "educational" film images of Africa and people of African ancestry, that it is difficult to avoid the conclusion that the conveyance of such a message seems to be the real intention of the U.S. educational system.

Especially at a time when racial tension and violence are escalating there is a serious need for interethnic communication and appreciation. As Baber and Gay contend:

> Although the United States is a culturally diverse and ethnically pluralistic society, most whites live in isolation from anything other than transient and superficial contacts with black Americans. When opportunities occur for whites to interact with blacks, the results are frequently disastrous. Either whites do not know what to do or how to behave, are uncomfortable and intimidated or, even worse, employ racially stereotypic attitudes and values. Unless whites learn to know and understand the black experience, and appreciate how their lives are affected by its presence and influence in American history, life, and culture, they will continue to look over, read past, ignore, minimize, or deny the human worth of black Americans. (Baber and Gay 1987:26)

IN SEARCH OF SOLUTIONS: SOME PRACTICAL GUIDELINES FOR EFFECTIVE CROSS-CULTURAL EDUCATION

Given this dismal reality, what can teachers do? A major implication of my 1980 analysis and 1991 follow-up study is that very few "educational" films can be shown alone to portray accurate views of Africans and peoples of

African ancestry. Most require a great deal of pre-viewing preparation and post-viewing discussion. Thus, conscientious teachers who want to teach a realistic view of the world have no choice but to assume personal responsibility for their own enlightenment to compensate for their systematic miseducation. On that basis, teachers can then pass along to their pupils a truly analytical and critical perspective.

According to Delancey (1977:20): "We must use audio-visual aids if we are to give our students a view of the realities of Africa, but we must select and use such materials with great care. Those who produce and sell such items must become more sensitive to the subtle and pervasive influence of racial superiority and white smugness that seems to arise in many of the goods they sell." Arguing that teachers must accept responsibility for using such materials intelligently, Delancey suggests that "properly prepared materials can overcome rather than abet racist attitudes" (1977:20). Should poorly prepared films that "repeat the old myths" about Africa and people of African descent be just thrown away, then? Delancey indicates some imaginative ways in which interested and skillful teacher can use these films constructively and creatively.

A film strip might be more useful if the teacher were to prepare a narration and discard the narration provided. Or, the teacher might show the strips and play the narration, stopping where appropriate to point out or to discuss the reasons for such inaccuracies. A teacher could use such materials in an effort to make students aware of racism and the subtle ways it infuences our thoughts. (Delancey 1977:20)

Teachers and school districts can play a major role in encouraging filmmakers and distributors to portray responsible images by carefully screening materials and selecting for purchase only those that live up to justifiable standards such as those mandated by documents such as California's *Framework*. However, it is unrealistic to expect most teachers who might use these materials to have the kind of knowledge base and experiences that would allow them to evaluate and use such films critically because they themselves are products of the same educational system and participants in the same mass media culture in which such images are the norm. In addition, most teachers assume that the educational materials provided for their use have been created by qualified experts and have undergone a rigorous selection process before being purchased—whether or not these assumptions conform to reality. Thus they generally feel confident about using these materials.

Unfortunately, in the hands of other than a critically thinking teacher with a sensitivity to and respect for the value and values of other people's lifestyles, the great majority of "educational" films on Africa and the African Diaspora are pernicious. Rather than inculcating an appreciation for the lives and lifestyles of others, these films, with a few exceptions, present an unbalanced, disparagingly Eurocentric view of the lives of the people of Africa and African ancestry. Consequently, they do more harm than good, and any positive value of their use, other than to provoke a critical discussion of ways of presenting and promoting ethnocentrism, is highly questionable. To use the available films on Africa and people of African ancestry intelligently and constructively, teachers must be conscious of

Why such negative images were created in the first place and why they continue to be perpetuated by Euro-American society in spite of the plethora of available information to the contrary.
How these images are conveyed, that is, the specific features of the images.
What the implications are for African Americans and for Euro-Americans of seeing Africans and African Americans consistently portrayed in negative ways.
Why these negative images continue to be taught in the schools at all.

It is imperative that teachers be able to understand the issues, judge films based on enlightened criteria, and use such films critically and intelligently in order to present the real issues to all children—African American and non-African American. The questions and issues raised in this process should sensitize teachers of different ethnic and cultural orientations to think critically about their own and others' attitudes toward, and evaluation of, images of other people's cultures in the world in a more general sense.

Furthermore, teachers must be able to do the following:

- *Separate myths from reality*: However subtle myths or generally negative images are presented—via explicit words, implications, or visual images—teachers should point them out to students, explaining any inaccuraies and misrepresentations and discussing how they came to be and why they are perpetrated.
- *Explain the meaning of unfamiliar issues raised in films*: This is especially important for those issues and other elements of African and other non-Western lifestyles that, if left unexplained, could lead to misunderstanding.
- *Explain the kinds of relationship—historical, economic, political, cultural, and the like—that Africa and the African Diaspora have with each other and with other parts of the world:* This would include discussion of issues such as slavery, missionary evangelism, colonialism and neocolonialism, international trade, political independence struggles, African cultural retentions in the Americas, and other aspects.
- *Situate the films in their proper historical context*: This is especially important given that so many public school film library holdings on Africa and the African Diaspora are dated.

The principles of the *Framework* directly inspired the following guidelines for teaching history and social science in the public schools and so are discussed in more depth.

Encourage Constant Questioning and Examination

Here are some sample questions that can be asked and answered in classroom discussion to stimulate the critical thinking process that is integral to the successful viewing of films on Africa and the African Diaspora:

- Do you learn how the people in question see themselves and what they themselves think about their lifestyle?
- How is this information conveyed? (For example, do the subjects of the film have the opportunity to talk about and for themselves, or do you only learn the filmmakers' views of them through narration?)
- What do you think was the filmmakers' intent in making the film?
- How do filmmakers portray the people in question—respectfully or not? Do you think the people in question would feel that their way of life has been portrayed accurately? What would they think of the perspective chosen from which to view it, and would they approve of the images shown and the issues chosen for exploration?
- How is the portrayal done (e.g., choice of images, use obvious or subtle language in narration)?
- What aspects of life are portrayed (e.g., problematic or normal issues)? Is the lifestyle folklorized or exoticized?

Discussion of Common Misconceptions

Teachers do not have to become experts on Africa or the African Diaspora to effectively teach students about these topics. Teachers can compensate for their lack of detailed knowledge by pointing out common misconceptions that surround these areas and by urging students to discuss and question them. For example, Africa is often described in such a way that it is viewed as a single, homogeneous country. It is therefore imperative that teachers establish, first for themselves and then for their students, the individuality and diversity of the various countries, regions, and ethnic groups of Africa.

Geographical facts are often the first and only information U.S. students learn about Africa, and frequently become the sole topic of discussion. Teachers can put geographical information into perspective by presenting it in a sociocultural context (e.g., discussing rivers and deserts in reference to their roles in the lives of the surrounding human communities). Teachers should also discuss the hundreds of different languages found on the African continent, as well as those spoken by people of African ancestry throughout the Diaspora. They should be especially careful when discussing unfamiliar social and cultural institutions such as African religious and family systems, and should explain the logic of unfamiliar institutions such as polygamy.

African and other cultures are often dismissed as primitive and underdeveloped due primarily to Americans' lack of understanding of them and tendency to evaluate them by contemporary U.S. criteria rather than their own. Greater effort to comprehend the unfamiliar aspects of these cultures will inevitably lead to greater appreciation of their worth. Thus, aspects of African societies should be evaluated as much as possible according to the criteria of their own cultures. It is, of course, useful to compare institutions from one society to those of another for the purpose of demonstrating the different, interesting, valid ways in which humans can configure reality. Such comparisons, however, must be made in a nonjudgmental manner; teachers should avoid adopting a Eurocentric perspective and should not try to fit aspects of African culture into the framework of American society.

Americans often assume that Africans have no history simply because written evidence is not accessible. This misconception should be countered with a discussion of the rich and unique oral tradition of Africa and the African Diaspora. Literature should be reinterpreted to include the contributions of the oral tradition. This discussion should also point out that there has long been more than enough written information available to those who have chosen to seek it out and use it to provide accurate images.[3] The brief, century-long colonial history of Africa is usually presented from a Eurocentric point of view, with emphasis on the European positive contributions to Africa. To counter this bias, teachers should encourage students to try to evaluate European imperialism and colonialism from an African stance and not ignore colonialism's often destructive impact on millennial African cultures and socioeconomic systems. In addition, African resistance to colonization, and cultural resiliency in the face of it, should be highlighted.

Teachers should help their pupils try to imagine themselves living in an African society so as to try to understand its institutions from the inside—according to the African cultural logic on which they are based rather than their own. Teachers and students should try to imagine themselves living in the society about which they are trying to learn and then decide how they would want to be portrayed. The resulting empathy combined with the previously mentioned themes and techniques can enable even those with limited knowledge to effectively teach about Africa and the African Diaspora.

Videotape series such as Basil Davidson's 1984 eight-part *Africa: Anatomy of a Continent* and Ali Mazrui's 1986 nine-part public television series *The Africans: A Triple Heritage* both offer a wealth of well-analyzed information about the history, social realities, and evolution of the continent. Mazrui's series, designed as a college level telecourse, is accompanied by a companion volume, a reader, and a study guide (Mazrui 1986a, 1986b, 1986c), all of which are extremely useful for educational purposes. Such videotape series, though too sophisticated for K-12 school audiences, could provide useful tools for teacher self-education

CONCLUSIONS

Papers presented at the 1979 Images of Africa Conference focused on the persistent idea of Euro-American superiority to Africans, and on the prejudicial and often inaccurate terminology used in describing African life. Forward-looking thinkers and educators have long maintained that an educational process that teaches truth—as opposed to one that advances pseudoscientific interpretations of distorted facts—can only be created by instilling cross-cultural awareness and an appreciation of diversity. This point is continually reiterated in the California *History/Social Studies Framework*, yet the model district's film collection provides convincing evidence of a systematically antithetical perspective. My 1980 and 1991 reviews of educational film holdings in this and other public school districts reveal that despite the fact that Africa is now a continent of independent nations, accurate portrayals of this reality remain virtually absent from the contemporary images of the continent to which U.S. schoolchildren are exposed.

As a result of the dearth of accurate and sensitive educational media about Africa and the African Diaspora, teachers must bear what may seem to be more than their share of the responsibility for offering effective education. The recommended actions and approaches suggested in this chapter are quite general and are intended primarily to help begin the reorientation of attitudes that is one of the biggest contributors to positive learning. Such efforts could go a long way in helping teachers first to expand their own worldviews and, by exension, to convey to students an appreciation for other peoples of the world— a goal that many educational planners reputedly view as desirable, while obviously condoning the use of instructional aids that do the contrary. Thus, the major task for teachers is to work to actualize the idealized principles that school districts proclaim, but as this educational media analysis suggests they are falling sorely short of this objective.

NOTES

1. When some participants at the Images of Africa Conference resolved to lodge a formal complaint with film and television producers and distributors about the continued projection of Tarzan films, many conferees thought the idea of such a protest anachronistic in an era in which most of Africa was constituted of independent nations. During the two years following the conference, however, two new Tarzan films were released. In a continuation of America's most consistent cinematic denigration of Africans—and by extension, of all people of African ancestry—Tarzan films continue to be shown on television.

2. Adjaye further contends that in recent years the media have overemphasized those African nations that are periodically drought-stricken giving an uninformed public the impression that famine and starvation are representative of the continent. Thus creating yet another overly generalized, unrepresentative, and distressing image of Africa has been created.

3. A major issue of which teachers and everyone else concerned about accurate education concerning Africa and the African Diaspora should be aware is that there already exists a substantial body of critical and constructive literature concerning the topic. The reference list accompanying this chapter serves as a guide for teachers in that it includes references to critiques and reviews of existing materials, guidelines, and criteria for evaluating mateirals, and sources of further information. The 1990 Rockefeller report, for example, in addition to its own findings and references to literature about the topic, includes the addresses of university-based Africa Outreach Programs that have as their mission the goal of helping educate the public about the continent.

REFERENCES

Adjaye, J. 1979. Media on Africa: Problems and Related Strategies with Reference to the Elementary Curriculum. Paper presented at the Images of Africa in the Media Conference, African Studies Center, Michigan State University, East Lansing, Mich.

Anosinke, B. 1982. Africa and Afro-Americans: the Bases for Greater Understanding and Solidarity. *Journal of Negro Education* 51(4): 434-438.

Asia in American Texts. 1976. New York: Asia Society.

Baber, C. and Gay, G. 1987. Black Studies for White Students—A Critical Need. *Momentum,* February: 26-28.

Beyer, B.K. 1968. Selected Materials for Teaching Africa South of the Sahara in American Secondary Schools: A Survey and a Challenge. *African Studies Review* 11:18-32.

Black Experience: A Selected List of 16mm Films for Program Planners. 1971. Boston: Boston Public Library.

Bohannon, P. 1964. *The Myth and the Fact: Africa and Africans.* New York: Doubleday and Co. Reprinted in R.A. Maynard ed., *Africa on Film: Myth and Reality.* Rochelle Park, N.J.: Hayden Book Co. pp. 1-7.

Butler, J. E. 1972. Audiovisual Aids for the Study of Africa: A Selected Guide to New Materials for Children and Young Adults. *A Current Bibliography on African Affairs* 5: 185-199.

California State Department of Education. *History/Social Science Framework for Public Schools.* 1981. Sacramento: California State Department of Education.

———.1988. Sacramento: California State Department of Education.

Cortés, C.E. 1983. Multiethnic and Global Education: Partners for the Eighties? *Phi Delta Kappan* 65(8): 568-571.

Crane, L. 1983. Some Guidelines for Evaluating Materials about Africa for Children. In *Curriculum Materials for Teachers.* Urbana: University of Illinois Press, pp. 71-74.

Curtin, P.D. 1964. *The Image of Africa.* Madison: University of Wisconsin Press.

Davidson, B. 1984. *Africa: A Voyage of Discovery.* Eight-part video series, MBT/RM Arts and Channel 4 Co-Production.

Delancey, M.W. 1977. Visual Aids for Teaching about Southern Africa. In N.J. Schmidt, ed. *Children's Literature and Audio-Visual Materials on Africa.* Buffalo, N.Y.: Conch Magazine Limited.

Dumor, C. 1979. Audio-Visual Sources of African Literature for Children K-8. Paper presented at the Images of Africa in the Media Conference, African Studies Center, Michigan State University, East Lansing, Mich.

Dunn, R.E. 1974. To the Editor (*New York Times*). Reprinted in R.A. Maynard ed., *Africa on Film: Myth and Reality.* Rochelle Park, N.J.: Hayden Book Co. p. viii.

Film Evaluations. 1979. Palo Alto, Calif.: Stanford University, Africa Education Project.

Gentemann, K. and Whitehead, T. 1983. The Cultural Broker Concept in Bicultural Education. *Journal of Negro Education* 52 (2): 118-128.

Hall, S. J. 1977. *Africa in U.S. Educational Materials: Thirty Problems and Responses.* New York: African-American Institute, School Services Division.

Hanvey, R.G. n.d. *An Attainable Global Perspective*. New York: Center for Global Perspectives.
Harrison, J.A. 1979. Improving the Quality of Audio-Visual Holdings in a State System of Education. Paper presented at the Images of Africa in the Media Conference, African Studies Center, Michigan State University, East Lansing, Mich.
Hilliard, A.G. III. 1978. On Equal Educational Opportunity and Quality Education. *Anthropology and Education Quarterly* 9(2): 110–126.
If It's Africa, This Must Be a Tribe. 1990. *Africa News*, p. 13.
The Image of the Middle East in Secondary School Texts. 1975. New York: Middle East Studies Association.
Jacqz, J. W. 1967. *Informing Americans about Africa*. New York: African-American Institute.
Maynard, R.A. 1974. *Africa on Film: Myth and Reality*. Rochelle Park, N.J.: Hayden Book Co.
Mazrui, A. 1986a. *The Africans: A Reader*. New York: Praeger Publishers.
———. 1986b. *The Africans: A Study Guide*. New York: Praeger Publishers.
———. 1986c. *The Africans: A Triple Heritage*. Boston: Little, Brown and Co.
———. 1986d. *The Africans: A Triple Heritage*. Nine-part PBS series, Wilmette, Ill.: Annenberg/CPB Collection.
Media special [Special issue]. 1990. *Africa News*.
Onipede, O. 1974. Hollywood's Holy War Against Africa. In R.A. Maynard ed., *Africa on Film: Myth and Reality*. Rochelle Park, N.J.: Hayden Book Co., pp. 72–75.
Patterson, L. 1974. In Movies, Whitey is Still King. In R.A. Maynard ed., *Africa on Film: Myth and Reality*. Rochelle Park, N.J.: Hayden Book Co., pp. 75–80.
President's Commission on Foreign Language and International Studies. *Strength Through Wisdom: A Critique of U.S. Capability*. 1979. Washington, D.C.: U.S. Government Printing Office.
Rashid, H. 1984. Promoting Biculturalism in Young African-American Children. *Young Children,* January:13–23.
Rich, E.J. 1974. Mind Your Language. *Africa Report*, September–October: 47–49.
———. 1979. Icons, Images, Ideas About Africa—What Is the Message? Paper presented at the Images of Africa in the Media Conference, African Studies Center, Michigan State University, East Lansing, Mich.
Rich, E.J., Rényi, J., and Friedrich, L. 1990. *A Greater Voice for Africa in the Schools: A Report Prepared for Rockefeller Foundation*. New York: The Rockefeller Foundation.
Rodney, W. 1974. *How Europe Underdeveloped Africa*. Washington, D.C.: Howard University Press.
Samoff, J. 1980. Tarzan, Terrs, and Liberation: A Challenge to Teachers Using Films on Africa. *Teaching Political Science* 8(1): 41–60.
Schmidt, N.J. 1975. *Children's Books on Africa and Their Authors: An Annotated Bibliography*. New York: Africana Publishing Co.
———.1979. Media to Teach about Africa in Grades K-8: An Overview. Paper presented at the Images of Africa in the Media Conference, African Studies Center, Michigan State University, East Lansing, Mich.
———.1979. *Supplement to Children's Books on Africa and Their Authors: An Annotated Bibliography*. New York: Africana Publishing Co.

———.1980. Criteria for Evaluating Precollegiate Teaching Materials on Africa. *Issue* 3(4): 58–60.

———.1981. *Children's Fiction about Africa in English*. Buffalo, N.Y.: Conch Magazine, Limited.

———.1990. Africans as Primary Actors in Their Own Lives and Lands: Validating African Curriculum Materials. Paper presented at the African Studies Association Meeting, Baltimore, Maryland.

Selected Black Studies Resources for Elementary Schools. n.d. Edison, N.J.: New Jersey Institute for the Study of Black Society and History and the New Jersey Urban Education Corps.

Szykowny, R. 1990. Bewildering the Herd. *The Humanist*, November–Dececember: 8–17.

Wiley, D.S. ed. 1982. *Africa on Film and Videotape, 1960–1981: A Compendium of Reviews*. East Lansing: African Studies Center, Michigan State University.

Wiley, M. 1979. "Media to Teach about Southern Africa in Secondary and Community Education." Paper presented at the Images of Africa in the Media Conference, African Studies Center, Michigan State University, East Lansing, Mich.

Wiley, M. and Zekiros, A. 1977. *Africa in Social Studies Textbooks*. Madison, Wis.: Department of Public Instruction.

Woodson, C. G. 1969. *The Mis-Education of the Negro*. Washington, D.C.: Associated Publishers. (Original work published in 1933).

CHAPTER 4

Why Blacks Are Committed to Blackness

Rhett S. Jones

If race is a useless construct for understanding human behavior, why is it that so many African Americans in general and African-American intellectuals in particular remain committed to it? This chapter explores the historical roots of blackness. Blackness is similar to ethnicity in that it marks one group off from another, has a distinct set of cultural traits, and those who share it believe they are related. But blackness is both more narrow and more broad than ethnicity. It is more narrow in that it has its origin in the unique experience of Africans and persons of African descent in British North America. It is because blackness has been adopted by so many persons of African descent around the globe that it is more broad than ethnicity. Ethnicity is grounded in a particular geographical place, whereas blackness has become worldwide. This chapter examines the history of the one drop rule which holds that any person of known African ancestry, regardless of her or his physical appearance, is black. While every nation in the western hemisphere includes persons of African descent, the one drop rule exists only in the United States. If the roots of blackness are found partly in widespread acceptance of the one drop rule, they are also partly found in the perceived absence of ethnicity among African Americans and most importantly in slavery. Lacking a sense of ethnicity and confronted with the one drop rule, the slaves created open communities. The chapter concludes that not only should African Americans continue their commitment to blackness, but also other Americans might do well to join them in adopting the behavior associated with it.

INTRODUCTION

Solomon Katz (1995) began a recent paper on race as follows:

Throughout this century many misconceptions about race have led to forms of racism that have caused much social, psychological and physical harm to many humans throughout the world. Unfortunately, a substantial part of these misconceptions have had their origins in various papers and books that depend heavily on old and outmoded biological concepts of race. However, as the analysis presented in this paper today will demonstrate, the changing concepts of what constitutes race have now developed to the point where the old biological concepts of race no longer provide scientifically valid distinctions.

Katz presented his paper as a member of a panel sponsored by the American Association for the Advancement of Science entitled *Is Race a Legitimate Concept in Science?* The panel, composed of scholars from the physical and social sciences, and the humanities, agreed that there was no biological basis for race as the term is commonly understood. At about the same time the panelists were preparing their papers, a number of scholars were criticizing Herrnstein and Murray's *The Bell Curve* (1994) for its reliance on scientifically discredited ideas about the racial basis of intelligence.

Definitions of ethnicity and blackness must be understood in order to examine this committment to blackness. By ethnicity is meant the array of cultural traits that make a group unique and distinct from other groups. Ethnicity usually involves a shared sense of history and a belief that those sharing an ethnic heritage are biologically linked to one another. Whether a biological relationship exists may or may not be true; what is important is that those who constitute the ethnic group believe there is a biological tie. At first glance, blackness appears to be like ethnicity in that it marks one group off from another, has a distinct set of cultural traits, and those who share it believe they are related. But blackness is grounded in the experiences of Africans and persons of African descent in British North America. While persons of African descent in other parts of the world have adopted and accepted the idea of blackness, it had its beginnings in the thirteen colonies. It is because blackness has been adopted by so many persons of African descent around the globe that it is more broad than ethnicity. Ethnicity is grounded in a particular geographical place, whereas blackness has become worldwide.

Blackness, like race itself, is a social construct, and like race it has no genetic basis. Blackness is instead a normative and behavioral system, a way of looking at the world reflecting, deciding on how one ought to behave, and then acting accordingly. Its roots are in the slave experience, and for that reason blackness is unique. Neither whiteness nor ethnicity is conceptually like blackness. Blackness is rooted in the one drop rule, in the absence of ethnicity among African Americans, and in the slave experience.

BLACKNESS AND THE ONE DROP RULE

The one drop rule holds that any person of known African ancestry, regardless of his or her physical appearance, is black. The one drop rule has two distinct characteristics. First, although virtually every nation in the Western Hemisphere includes persons of African descent, the one drop rule exists only in the United States. In all other American nations and the European colonies that preceded them, miscegenation was acknowledged by the creation of an elaborate racial hierarchy consisting, for example, of mulattos (persons of mixed European and African ancestry), mestizos (persons of mixed European and Native American ancestry), and a host of other types intended to measure and reflect the amount and sources of racial intermixture (Mellafe 1975; Morner 1967; Rout 1976). Persons were not simply placed in categories, but these categories were ranked. So, for example, mulattos had access to jobs that were closed to blacks, whereas Indians were exempt from the persecution of the Inquisition and mestizos were not. These racial terminologies were incorporated in the cultures of the new American settlements, manifesting themselves in stereotypes that in their turn had an impact on race relations.

Because the United States and the thirteen colonies of British North American that preceded its formation were not isolated from the rest of the Americas, some of this terminology acknowledging race mixture soon found itself into American ideas about race. So, for example, most Americans understand that a mulatto is of mixed African and European ancestry. In his 1918 book, *The Mulatto in the United States,* sociologist Edward B. Reuter met most Euro-American expectations about race in arguing that virtually all Afro-American leaders were mulattos. To buttress his case he included numerous photographs showing that the majority of black leaders were partly European in ancestry. Despite Reuter's book and the on and off willingness of the United States Census to acknowledge racial intermixture, most Americans accept the one drop rule.

Ideas about miscegenation exist on the fringes of American racial consciousness. Sometimes these ideas reflect the continuation of racial attitudes that preceded the acceptance of the one drop rule in certain geographical locales. In New Orleans, for example, ideas about race continue to reflect the long control of the city and its environs by Spanish and the French settlers, both of whom acknowledged miscegenation in their racial terminology (Woods 1972). Similarly, the one drop rule was long rejected by the settlers of Charleston, South Carolina who brought with them racial categories developed in the British West Indies (Koger 1985). Similarly, most Euro-Americans know that the "half-breed" is a person of part white and Indian ancestry, and almost all who know the term accept the stereotype that half-breeds are a drunken, degenerate folk, embodying the worst characteristics of both races. But few know the term *zambo*. In many of the Spanish-speaking republics the *zambo* is a person of mixed Native American and African ancestry, but there is no equivalent term in the United States, thereby demonstrating the power of the one drop rule. For if there had been any significant social and sexual contact between Indians and blacks, a term would exist to refer to the children of these sexual relationships. None does.

The absence of the term *zambo* makes clear the second characteristic of the one drop rule, namely, it is applied only to blacks. One may be part Asian, or part Latino, but one may not be part black. Under the one drop rule, to be part black is to be entirely black. Sociologist F. James Davis, in *Who Is Black?* (1991), demonstrates that while all other American racial groups are regarded as assimilating minorities, blacks are not. The model for Latinos, Asians, and Native Americans is that of European "ethnics" who are accepted by European Americans to the extent that they willingly divest themselves of their Old World ethnic and cultural markers, thereby demonstrating their willingness to become Americans. While millions of black Americans have, over the centuries, demonstrated their willingness to accept the Euro-American way of life, blacks are not regarded as an assimilating minority. It is possible for a white candidate for political office in an attempt to attract the Indian vote, to make mention of her Native-American grandmother. It is possible for her to be both white and part Native American at the same time. But it is not possible for a white candidate, in an attempt to attract the black vote, to make mention of her African-American grandmother. If she has a black grandmother, under the one drop rule, she is black.

Scholars differ over the origins of the one drop rule. Historian Winthrop Jordan (1968) argues that the English attitude toward Africans was deeply rooted in their culture's ancient fear and loathing of the color black. In the English worldview, blackness was associated with the night, with dirt, and with evil. Psychologist Joel Kovel (1970) concludes that whites associated the dark skin color of blacks with feces and therefore had a basic aversion to persons of African descent. Psychologist Frances Welsing (1970) agreed with Kovel that the source of racism and hence of the one drop rule was to be found deep in the psychohistory of whites, but found it was based not in rejection of blackness, but in envy of it. Unable to produce melanin—the genetic factor that gives skin its color—Northern Europeans were envious of Africans and others who could. While doing everything possible to blacken themselves, they nevertheless created a worldwide system in which darker persons were punished, exploited, oppressed, and, in the case of Africans, enslaved. If the arguments of Jordan, Kovel, and Welsing are accepted, then the origin of the one drop rule is found in the long, deep, and complex interplay of European culture, psychology, and history.

Afrocentrists also find the origin of the one drop rule deep in the past, but in that of Africa, not of Europe. Historian Sterling Stuckey (1987), for example, writes of the direct and continuing link between the cultures of Central and West Africa and African-American culture. Research by Stuckey and other Afrocentrists (Asante 1988; Boateng 1993) suggests that, contrary to a widely held scholarly assumption, the cruelties of the Middle Passage and slavery did not destroy the African sense of self. The origin of the one drop rule is therefore found in the continuation of a felt African identity among African Americans. Afrocentrists argue that this sense of blackness is not rooted in racial essentialism and that African Americans include within their community persons who, though of African descent, are also the descendants of Native Americans, Europeans, and Asians. Afrocentrists further argue that West African cultures have historically been characterized by their willingness to incorporate and accept persons of different religious, economic, and political beliefs. Typically, West African ethnic groups incorporated into their pantheon of belief the gods and religious worldviews of persons they conquered. While African Americans constructed a social order open to persons of various racial mixture, at the same time they retained among themselves a sense of Africanity which made them willing partners in the construction of the one drop rule.

The work of three historians (Bennett 1970; Morgan 1975; Fredrickson 1981) suggests that the origin of the one drop rule is found in neither the ancient history of Africa nor that of Europe, but rather in the need of the 17th-century ruling class of British North America to control the growing slave population and its fear that slaves would ally themselves with lower class whites. According to Morgan: "If [white] freemen with disappointed hopes should make common cause with slaves of desperate hope the results [would be disastrous to ruling class whites.] The answer to the problem, obvious if unspoken and only gradually recognized, was racism, to separate dangerous free whites from dangerous slave blacks by a screen of racial contempt" (1975:328). As Bennett, Morgan and Fredrickson see it the roots of the one drop rule are to be found in the straightforward efforts of a 17th-century ruling class to maintain and extend its hegemony.

Mechal Sobel (1987) believes that race relations in colonial North America led to the one drop rule, but finds its origin not in the 17th-century, but the 18th. For much of the 18th century, she argues, whites from the lower orders of England and Africans found much in common. Both, for example, shared the idea that time was cyclical and repetitive, not linear, and an assumption that physical space had both sacred and secular characteristics. These and other shared worldviews drew them together against an emergent white elite holding a sense of time that was linear, and believing that space should be divided into sacred and secular arenas. Sobel titled her book *The World They Made Together*, thereby suggesting that—contrary to views held by scholars who assume there were always two distinct race-based cultures in British North America—for nearly two hundred years, the gulf was not between black and white, but instead between elite whites on the one hand, and other whites and blacks on the other.

This shared cultural orientation was reinforced by the practical needs of poor whites, poor blacks, and slaves to work together. Sobel writes:

Other whites, too, had business relationships with slaves both legal and illegal. Many blacks and whites worked out symbiotic relationships: blacks took plantation produce and exchanged it with poor whites for drink and hard goods. Poor whites were often dependent on this cheap source of provender. Upper class whites knew this and were determined to separate them. [George] Washington, for example recognized that without "their connexion [sic] with my Negroes," local poor whites "would be unable to live on the miserable land they occupy." Evidence of black-white partnerships in crime is widely available. (1987:50-51)

Washington, Thomas Jefferson, and other southern slaveholders did more than fret over these relations between whites and blacks; they did all they could to prevent and disrupt them.

A number of scholars conclude that the ideology of the American revolution with its insistence on the equality of man led to the one drop rule. If all men were created equal, then slaves ought to be freed. A. Leon Higginbotham (1980) is among those (Bailyn 1967; Jones 1978; Kaplan 1973) who suggests that the revolutionary generation could find no way out of this dilemma but to suggest that if all men were created equal, then blacks were not men. Higginbotham (1980:381-383) points out that Thomas Jefferson's original draft of the Declaration of Independence concluded with a significant diatribe against King George III for his encouragement of the slave trade. Higginbotham notes that, while this draft condemned the slave trade, it did not criticize American slavery itself. But this fine distinction, written after all by a slaveholder, was itself soon rendered meaningless. The approved and final draft made mention of neither the slave trade nor slavery. Wood outlines the dilemma facing the revolutionary generation: "Americans now recognized that slavery in a republic of workers was an aberration, 'a peculiar institution,' and that if any Americans were to retain it, as southern Americans eventually did, they would have to explain and justify it in new racial and anthropological ways that their formal monarchical society never needed" (1992:186). Only in these ways could slavery and a democratic republic be reconciled. Africans and their African-American children were transformed into despicable folk, separate and apart from the rest of the human race, destined by God to serve whites, and to be forever inferior to them.

Davis (1991) believes that the one drop rule had its beginnings in neither ancient Europe or Africa, nor in 17th-century, 18th-century, or revolutionary America. Instead, he finds it contended with an American understanding of race which recognized racial intermixture until after the Civil War. In the post-Reconstruction era, his argument runs, white Southerners who had exercised political and economic control over blacks by means of slavery were faced with the problem of how to continue to dominate blacks. It was at this point that the one drop rule was created, thereby providing an ideological justification for Jim Crow. Whites, even southern whites, did not everywhere and immediately accept the one drop rule, any more than they accepted legal segregation. Both not only imposed inconveniences on whites—restricting them as much as blacks were restricted—but also sometimes created pain by requiring them to deny family members and transform genuine friendships into relationships circumscribed by the emergent Jim Crow system.

In reaching this conclusion, Davis drew on C. Vann Woodward's *The Strange Career of Jim Crow* (1957). In the book, first published in 1955, Woodward clearly demonstrated that contrary to much American thinking, legal segregation was a recent invention dating only back to the 1890s and had been established within the living memory of many white Southerners. The book stirred up angry controversy in the South where it was widely assumed that the Jim Crow laws dated from the earliest colonial settlements and reflected whites' ingrained and natural aversion to blacks. Woodward's book directly challenged this belief and suggested that segregation was a social and legal response to the emancipation of Afro-Americans. Born in Arkansas, Woodward apparently felt the pressure from his fellow white Southerners and softened his argument in the 1957 edition

In the first place, although the segregation system is relatively new, it is grounded upon theories and attitudes that are not at all new. It is a mistake to assume that the ideas of innate Negro inferiority and white supremacy originated along with the Jim Crow system, for they are much older. Segregation is, after all, only the latest phase in the long history of the white man's ways of fixing the Negro's status, his "place." Along with these practices, and in justification of them, there developed the old assumptions of Anglo-Saxon superiority and African inferiority, white supremacy and Negro subordination. In so far as segregation is based on these assumptions, therefore, it is based upon the old proslavery arguments and has remote roots in the slavery period. (1957: xi–xii)

Although Woodward probably wrote in response to attacks on his work by segregationists, he offers perhaps the best answer to the origin of the one drop rule by suggesting that Euro-Americans have long been fascinated by Afro-Americans, and therefore by the meaning of race.

The one drop rule did not, therefore, necessarily have its origins in ancient history, the 17th-century, the 18th-century, the revolutionary era, or in the 1890s. Its roots were paradoxically, though understandably, in all of these as the white men and women who settled North America grappled with the black men and women they enslaved. These same whites also killed Native Americans by the thousands and discriminated against persons of many and diverse racial, religious, and ethnic backgrounds. Yet they found room for all of these peoples, for the Irish, the Italians, the Jews, the Chinese, the Chicanos, and Indians, allowing them to behave as—in Davis' terms—assimilating minorities and never applying the one drop rule to them.

Whatever its beginnings, the one drop rule played a powerful and central role in shaping blackness. It persuaded and convinced Americans of African descent that they were indeed a separate, distinct, but not inferior people. David Walker in his 1829 *Appeal to the Coloured Citizens of the World* (1965:12) argued that whites "think because they hold us in their infernal chains of slavery, that we wish to be white or of their color—but they are dreadfully deceived—we wish to be just as it pleased our Creator to have made us."

Walker accepted the concept of blackness and the one drop rule as did most African Americans of his era and of the generations that preceded it.

BLACKNESS AND ETHNICITY IN NORTH AMERICA

If the roots of blackness are found partly in widespread acceptance of the one drop rule, they are also found partly in the absence of ethnicity among African Americans. Every other group migrating to North America, as well as the American Indians who were already present, had an ethnic base for responding to what was an unprecedented experience. A number of scholars have objected to the term *New World* to refer to the evolution of the Americas in the wake of Columbus' voyages, but in fact the world was a new one in the sense that for the first time large numbers of persons of strikingly different physical appearance and cultural assumptions were thrown together. In Europe, even during the Age of Discovery, the vast majority of persons seldom traveled more than 40 miles from their birthplace in their entire lives. Within this circumscribed space, they generally encountered persons who looked like themselves, and such differences as did appear were explained by class, family, and sometimes religious factors. Peasants expected the gentry to behave in ways different from themselves, and Catholics expected Protestants to operate with a different set of assumptions.

C. Loring Brace (1995) attributes the rise of racial thought to the advances in European shipbuilding which made possible long voyages. As long as persons traveled overland from Europe, whether they reached the Near East, North Africa, or even China, as did Marco Polo, they saw no sudden changes in the physical appearance of persons. But ocean voyages were quite different as Europeans sailed from familiar ports populated by persons much like themselves and disembarked in places inhabited by persons who were neither physically nor culturally like themselves. Struck by these differences, Europeans sought to explain them in ways that would enable them to accomplish their own mercantile, religious, and imperial goals. It was one thing to grapple with these strange new peoples in their own environment, from which one might always escape, and it was quite another to build a New World, distant from Europe, in which they had to be reckoned with. Native Americans were already present when the colonists arrived, and the settlers soon transported Africans.

In understanding the role of ethnicity in the development of North America, it is important first to appreciate the achievements of the settlers. Much recent scholarship has denigrated their accomplishments, reading history backward and finding them to be racist, cruel and selfish oppressors, when in fact it makes far better sense to view them in terms of the challenges they met and mastered from the earliest settlements in the 17th-century to the time their European-American descendants declared independence from Great Britain. The colonists met and overcame, in turn, environmental, social, and cultural challenges (Jones 1988:31–33). Ethnicity played an important role in meeting each of these challenges.

The settlers first had to master the challenge presented by the environment. They had to learn which of their own crops would grow in North America, which of their animals could survive, and which native American plants and animals could safely be eaten. They solved these problems, partly by trial and error, partly by observing the Indians, and partly by deliberate instruction from them. In the southern colonies English settlers also learned much from imported African slaves who, for example, shared information on the cultivation of rice with their owners. The settlers literally built a New World as they constructed homes, buildings, roads, bridges, and churches. In so doing they transformed the environment. In this transformation ethnicity played a crucial role as the European immigrants learned from one another. Frequently, they built on one another's successes and learned from each other's failures. When the English took over New York, they profited from the knowledge the Dutch had gained in their dealings with Native Americans, just as the Dutch themselves had earlier learned from the settlers of New Sweden. Ethnic and related religious factors sometimes led to rejection of lessons learned by earlier settlers. So, for example, while the English were willing to take advantage of established Dutch relations with American Indians, they did not adopt the Dutch practices in which blacks were accorded a "half freedom" whereby they were routinely freed, held full church membership, and were free both to marry and to hold property (Higginbotham 1980; McManus 1973). At the same time, while the English frequently lamented the success of French Catholics in North America in converting the Indians, contrasting it with their own failure, they were unwilling to adopt the practices used by French missionaries.

Ethnicity also played a central role in resolving the problem of creating a working social order, a society in which the settlers could live and have reasonable expectations as to what would happen to them and to their children in the future. There were no European models to help the colonists. Europe was fragmented and divided by religious and national hate and was often at war during the settlement of North America. Spain, France, England, Russia, and a number of other minor European powers fought for control of North America, and there was no conception of a multicultural society to bring them together. And yet the colonists had to get along with one another. The Puritan theocracy in parts of Massachusetts and Connecticut was challenged not only by Scots, Dutch, Germans, and other immigrants, but also by the children of the Puritans themselves who refused to accept it. The charter of the colony of Georgia forbade slavery, but English entrepreneurs, envious of the wealth realized by their slaveholding fellows in South Carolina soon agitated to have the charter amended to allow slavery. They were strongly opposed by settlers of German and Scots background who insisted that Georgia should remain a colony of free persons who worked for themselves and did not force slaves to work for them (Flanders 1933; Scarborough 1933). They lost, but ethnicity clearly played a central role in their struggle. Eventually, the colonists agreed that whiteness was more important than the ethnic and religious differences that divided them, but even after they, and their American-born children, agreed on the importance of whiteness, ethnicity continued to be an important factor.

Ethnicity was particularly important in the next problem facing the colonists who having mastered the environment and having established a set of working social relations, now had to legitimate these relations. Put in yet another way, having created a society, they now had to create a culture and thereby persuade themselves that the solutions they had devised were correct. Put in a still different way English settlers now sought to convince newly arrived migrants from Europe to accept the emergent Anglo-American patterns of life and the institutions that supported it. In multicultural colonies such as New York, Georgia, Pennsylvania, Rhode Island, and Maryland, this celebration of English ways was not widely accepted, but in what was to become an American pattern, ethnic communities opted for a two-pronged strategy. Insofar as possible, they recreated the institutions of their homeland, maintaining the language and supporting churches and cultural institutions. At the same time, immigrants accepted the Anglo-American political and economic order. Ethnicity remained important in the social and cultural lives of many of the people and was often turned to advantage in economic and political matters. Members of ethnic communities tended to do business with one another and to support elected officials and government policies that served the interest of their particular group. But while they remained culturally distinct from Anglo-Americans, such groups as the Irish, Germans, and Jews were drawn into the larger social framework of the nation and accepted its ideology. The much celebrated American melting pot existed only in the political and economic spheres. In marriage, in religion, and often in education and place of residence, ethnicity remained important.

The pushy aggressiveness of persons who were not white stimulated the growth of whiteness as a concept. Prior to the arrival of whites, control of a given area of land often shifted back and forth among Indian ethnic groups, always with the idea of maintaining harmony among the tribes themselves and with nature. But by the early 18th-century, it became clear to most Indians that there would be no give and take between themselves and the English; the colonists always took land, they never returned it. From this point on, some Indians became fierce foes of the settlers, while others sought to work with them in order to retain Indian land and an Indian way of life. The English and their Anglo-American children were aware of this resistance and understood that the basis for it was the Indian's commitment to his culture. Blacks were no less troublesome than the Indians, with whom they sometimes made common cause (Bateman 1990). They ran away, rebelled, and resisted in other ways. Fear of slave conspiracies was a staple of colonial thought, and even free blacks were seldom trusted. Collins (1985:66) concludes that "Indians and blacks together thus boosted whites' sense of unity and common purpose as well as their race pride."

While Native Americans may have solidified a sense of whiteness among the settlers, they presented a different set of problems to Englishmen and their Anglo-American children from that of European immigrants. At the time the whites arrived, Indians already possessed rich, complex cultures. From the perspective of the settlers, Indians could be persuaded to accept Anglo-American culture, they could be pushed out of spaces controlled by the colonists, or they could be destroyed. White American attitudes toward Indians evolved over time, reflecting both assumptions made about Native Americans and relations with them. Although Thomas (1975) argues that the Puritans, and by extension other 17th-century English colonists, were racist from the beginning and never intended to admit Indians as full members of their communities, a number of other scholars (Axtell 1981; Horsman 1981; McLoughlin 1986) conclude that many settlers sought to both civilize and Christianize Native Americans and to fully incorporate them into their settlements. Certainly, this was the attitude of Thomas Jefferson and other influential men. In the early years of the new republic, the federal government allotted funds and personnel, and encouraged missionary societies to work among the Indians in order to civilize them. But by the 1830s the Anglo-American attitude had changed. Indians were no longer regarded as capable of being assimilated despite the fact that a number of tribes, among them the Cherokee and the Seneca, had transformed their societies by adopting Anglo-American ways.

From the perspective of the Indians, the settlers presented both a problem in themselves and in their changing attitudes toward Native Americans. Dowd states that the Indians had two responses to the English colonization of North America:

Indians who identified with "tribal" leaders generally emphasized the interests of their particular people; these often cooperated with, although they were only rarely controlled by, the imperial powers. In the terms of this book, they were advocates of *accommodation*. Others cast their lot with the movement's militants, here termed *nativists*, holding less regard for "tribal" affiliation. Still others occupied positions between the two poles or shifted from one position to the other. (1993:xxi)

These two poles mirrored exactly the choices confronting the European immigrants. Indians could either seek to accommodate themselves to Anglo-American culture, or they could attempt to maintain their traditional way of life.

Like the European immigrants, Indians responded to this Anglo-American challenge along ethnic, or to use the more old-fashioned term, tribal lines. In the South, for example, the Cherokee and Seminole dealt with whites and white ideas about race and culture in different ways. The Seminole accepted Africans and African Americans as full members of the tribe. According to Littlefield:

For the most part the Seminole blacks lived like their masters and allies. They dressed Seminole fashion and lived in houses built of timbers and shingles lashed to posts and rafters with strips of oak. The men owned guns and supplemented their diet with game. Described as "stout and even gigantic" in comparison to the Indians, these blacks were more clever [in their dealings with whites] than their masters. Most spoke Spanish and English as well as the Indian languages. As a result, they were called upon more and more as interpreters and go-betweens when the Indians dealt with the whites. (1977:8)

The Second Seminole War was caused, in part, by the efforts of white Southerners to force Seminoles of African ancestry back into slavery on the grounds that they were the descendants of runaway slaves.

The Cherokee, regarded by many scholars as the most assimilated American Indians during the colonial and early national periods, took a very different attitude toward white American culture. Some, although not all of the Cherokee, rejected communal ownership of land in favor of individual farms, shifted farming from women's to men's work, ended the clan system, replaced traditional religious beliefs with Christianity, and changed a matrilineal system to a patrilineal one. The Cherokee also adopted a constitution modeled on that of the United States, created an alphabet, published a newspaper, and became slaveholders. Many of them also accepted Euro-American racism. Like most other peoples of the world the Cherokee had a set of Creation Myths, ideas about the origin of the world. Prior to the arrival of Europeans and their African slaves, these myths made no mention of race, but by the 1820s this had changed. In a myth collected in 1824 (McLoughlin et al. 1984:256–257), a Cherokee explained that the Great Spirit made the white, black, and red man but that all were destitute until they saw three large boxes descending from the sky.

Then the Great Spirit spoke and said, "White man, you are pale weak, but I made you first, and will give you the first choice; go to the boxes, open them and look in, and choose which you will take for your portion." The white man opened the boxes, looked in and said, "I will take this." It was filled with pens, and ink, and paper, and compasses, and such things as [white] people now use. The Great Spirit spoke again and said, "Black man, I made you next, but I do not like you. You may stand aside. The Red man is my favourite, he shall come forward and make the next choice; Red man, choose your portion of the things of this world." The red man stepped boldly up and chose a box filled with tomahawks, knives, war clubs, traps, and such things as are useful in war and hunting. The Great Spirit laughed when he saw how well his red son knew how to choose. Then he said to the negro, "You may have what is left, the third box is for you." That was filled with axes, and hoes, with buckets to carry water in, and long whips for driving oxen, which meant that the negro must work for both the red and white man, and it has been so ever since.

Prior to the arrival of Europeans, the Cherokee had a system of slavery, but it was not based on race. As this myth suggests, however, many of these Indians had now accepted racist rationalizations for slavery.

The Cherokee and other Native Americans did more than simply accept racist ideas and incorporate them in their myths; they also manipulated them with considerable skill. In a 1793 letter Little Turkey, a Cherokee chief sent to William Blount, then governor of Tennessee, the Spaniards were described as "a lying, deceitful, treacherous people, and not real white people, and what few I have seen of them looked like mulattos, and I would never have anything to say to them" (Perdue 1979:48). At the time Little Turkey wrote, the English, the French, the Spaniards, and the recently established American Republic were all attempting to gain control and influence over Indians in the southeastern part of what is now the United States. Just as these powers sought to play the Indians off against one another, so too did the Indians skillfully play them off against each other. Little Turkey may not therefore have believed the Spaniards were mulattos, but he knew enough about the prejudices of Anglo-Americans to pretend he did.

Indians did not always simply choose between maintaining their native traditions and wholeheartedly embracing European ones. Like the European immigrants, many tribes sought to temporize, to find a middle ground between their way of life and that of the invaders. Richter (1992:480) explains that the Protestant Mohawks of Tiononderoge had returned, after conversion to Christianity, to many traditional practices but "had not abandoned their faith as they defined it. They continued to pray to the Christian God and to teach their children lessons learned from [white missionaries] even while many also participated in ceremonial feasts, consulted traditionalist shamans, and fulfilled wishes expressed in each others' dreams." Like European immigrants both the Mohawks and other Native Americans were apart from and incorporated into Anglo-American culture, and like the immigrants they created a new identity for themselves. The colonists moved from a sense of their separate ethnic identity to agreement on the fact that they were white. Similarly, Dowd (1993:xv) argues that Indians "came to recognize commonality. Factions of them acted on that recognition, producing a movement as religious as it was political." He goes on to demonstrate that this pan-Indian movement of resistance was cross tribal and produced, at least among many Native Americans a sense that all Indians had something in common.

Yet ultimately both white peoples and Native Americans coped with the strange New World from an ethnic/tribal base. While Euro-Americans accepted the concept of whiteness and eventually celebrated it, many of them retained a sense of ethnicity, and from this ethnic base helped to shape whiteness. Similarly, Indians retained a strong sense of tribal identity while at the same time working to forge pan-Indian alliances. In committing themselves to these larger identities rooted in a sense of whiteness and Indianness, the two groups had to submerge their ethnic identities, yet these remained durable and strong.

The experience of blacks was different from that of all other Americans who coped with the emergent New World from an ethnic base. Slavery destroyed ethnicity among blacks. During the latter 17th and early 18th centuries, when African-American culture had its beginnings there were comparatively few blacks and it was rare indeed for a number of persons from the same ethnic group to be enslaved in the same area. The slaves had to cope with all the problems faced by their owners as they had to resolve a series of physical, social, and cultural challenges, but in addition they had to adjust to slavery, and perhaps most important of all, adjust to one another. Unlike Native Americans and European immigrants, the slaves were not able to bring intact, ethnic-based cultures with them to grapple with New World problems. They had to forge a new identity without having an ethnic base on which to draw.

In this the North American slave experience was distinct and different from the slave experience in English, French, and Spanish settlements in the Caribbean and parts of South America, and from Portuguese settlements in Brazil. In these colonies, large numbers of slaves from the same ethnic groups in West Africa were brought together under circumstances that enabled them not only to maintain their language, their customs, and a sense of their history, but also to pass this knowledge on to their American-born children. So, for example, it is possible to trace the history of the Fon in Haiti, the Ashanti and Fanti in Jamaica, and the Yoruba in Brazil. Murphy describes one African ethnic group in colonial Cuba:

The Yoruba were quick to establish a strong community in Havana. They came to be called "Lucumi" after their way of greeting each other, "*oluku mi*, imy friend." They formed guilds and dance halls, taverns, and fraternities, where they would dance the old dances. More than ever they needed [their gods] and their ways of power, and they found ingenious ways of keeping them alive. (1993:27)

With the change of a few words, this could well describe the experience of many other African ethnic groups in Latin America and the Caribbean, just as it could serve as an equally valid description of such ethnic groups as the Germans and the Irish in British North America.

It could not, however, serve as a description of the African experience in North America where the ethnic link between Africans and their Afro-American children was broken. In *The Myth of the Negro Past* (1941) Melville Herskovits proved, though many of the readers of his time, both white and black, rejected his proofs, that African culture had not been eliminated among New World blacks. What had been eliminated was the sense of ethnic continuity, so that Africa's children in North America lacked a sense of themselves as Yoruba, Ewe, or Fanti and knew only that they were black. In concluding the chapter poignantly entitled "The Death of the Gods," Albert Raboteau writes:

The character of the religious milieu, the average number of slaves on plantations, and the number of Africans in the slave population were all factors in the survival or loss of African culture. In the United States all these factors tended to inhibit the survival of African culture and religion. It was not possible to maintain the rites of worship, the priesthood, or the [ethnic] identities which were the vehicles and supports for African theology and cult organization. Nevertheless, even as the Gods of Africa gave way to the

God of Christianity, the African heritage of singing, dancing, spirit possession, and magic continued to influence Afro-American spirituals, ring shouts, and folk beliefs. (1980:92)

Africa continued to be important to black slaves in the thirteen colonies, although they were unable to retain a sense of ethnic identity.

African ethnicity played no role in the new sense of self built by North American blacks. While their task was no easy one, it was facilitated by two factors. First, most slaves were imported from West Africa, from a region roughly between the present-day African nations of Senegal and Angola, and areas near the Atlantic coast. Metraux (1972:29) explains the consequences, noting that most of these peoples "have basically a common culture in spite of linguistic differences and deep antagonisms. Resemblances were increased by reciprocal influence and frequent contact." This shared culture is best understood by comparing it to the shared culture of Western Europe where despite differences in religion, language, and governance there was a widespread acceptance of what constituted civilization, moral behavior, and widespread belief in Christianity. Second, in addition to sharing a common culture, African slaves had the common experience of creating ways of working with one another within the chains of slavery before they arrived in North America. In the slave pens and on the slave ships, Africans of different ethnic, class, and religious backgrounds learned to cooperate with one another. Their working understandings might be viewed as the beginning of the African-American culture in which ethnicity played no part. The slaves sometimes committed collective suicide by together jumping off ships; other times shortly after their arrival in the New World they revolted or ran away. They early understood the need to support one another, and they early understood what they shared. While Europeans and Native Americans were moving toward a sense of race that would transcend their ethnicity and draw them together, in the absence of ethnicity the slaves created and embraced blackness.

This is not the simple and oft-repeated argument that the slave experience was so horrible and overwhelming that Africans transported to the New World as slaves lost all vestiges of African cultures. Instead it is an argument that in the absence of ethnicity the slaves of North America were forced to draw on African cultures in a way that was unique in the hemisphere. In parts of Latin America and the Caribbean, African ethnicity remained so powerful that the slavemasters were able to play African ethnic groups off against one another by encouraging their distinct identities. But in the thirteen colonies of British North America all slaves were treated as though they were the same, and transported Africans themselves were forced to seek out cultural areas of commonality, which transcended the differences among African ethnic groups.

The slaves used their discovery of a shared West African culture in aggressive ways, defining the world in their terms and rejecting those of Anglo-Americans. As Issac writes:

Afro-Virginians cannot have been caught in the subtle tensions between church-centered, "sacred" celebrations and home-centered, "profane" forms. For them the English Christian distinctions between the "religious" and the "secular" would probably have had little meaning. Although we can discover almost nothing of the symbols that the slaves used to represent ultimate value and meaning, we know that their primary modes of expression were song and dance, with exemplary tales perhaps playing a secondary role. A basic African cultural "grammar" appears to have transcended the great diversities of language and specific customs that confronted the captive migrants as they began to coalesce into a distinct society upon the North American seaboard. This is a case where the medium was indeed the essence of the message. Clearly, during the formative decades of the eighteenth century the slaves were able to keep alive distinctive African expressive styles and sensibilities. (1982:70)

Afro-Virginians, Africans forcibly transported to Virginia, and their fellows in the other twelve colonies found ethnicity irrelevant and useless in their struggle and so moved beyond it. In rejecting ethnicity, they created blackness.

BLACKNESS AND SLAVERY

Blackness was rooted partly in the one drop rule, partly in the absence of ethnicity among North American blacks, but most importantly in slavery. Lacking a sense of ethnicity and confronted with the one drop rule, the slaves created open communities. Blackness was open to all who were slaves regardless of whether they physically appeared to be African, European, Native American, or, as was increasingly the case after the middle of the 18th century, some combination of the three. As they did not control their own communities, the slaves made a virtue out of necessity, and slave societies were open to all. They were populated by persons of varied African, European, and Native American heritage, but, because slavery was based on race in North America, all were considered black. Whites were never enslaved, and Native-American slavery had pretty much ended by the mid-18th century. Moreover, the emergent white American justification for slavery was the inferiority of Africans. It would have been unthinkable to enslave either whites or Indians so that all slaves were, by definition, black. While Euro-Americans were creating a sense of whiteness based on the alleged racial purity of white folk, Afro-Americans were creating a sense of blackness based, in part, on their shared slavery. Whiteness was ultimately based on the idea that all white people were linked together in a great chain of racial superiority over all nonwhites, while blackness was based on a sense that all black people were linked together by a shared experience in America's race-based slavery.

With scholars increasingly sensitive to the persecution of many of America's peoples—Native Americans, Chinese, Jews, Chicanos, Catholics, and many others—the oppression and suffering of African Americans is often regarded as essentially similar to that of other groups. In many American colleges courses on race and ethnicity are taught in which the two are viewed as much the same, and the black experience is discussed as one that is in the process of evolving through a number of stages similar to the stages through which European immigrant groups passed. Katz (1995) has suggested that ethnicity might eventually replace race as a more useful construct and one that has the advantage of being rooted in culture and not in some supposed, but—despite all the efforts made by racists—never identified set of genes. Katz is correct, and it makes sense to replace race with ethnicity as a way of exploring the history and culture of all other American groups except blacks. Blacks had a racial not an ethnic experience, an experience shaped by slavery.

Slaves had no rights and enjoyed none of the legal protections and other safeguards that all other Americans took for granted. The absence of these protections struck most deeply at the most basic of all human institutions, the family. With the exception of a brief period in the 17th century when the large number of African males imported as slaves were housed in barracks, most slaves lived in families consisting of father, mother, children, and on occasion members of the extended family. The slave family looked like every other American family, but appearances are deceiving. For each slave family had an invisible member, the slaveholder. It was the slaveholder who decided whether a man or a woman who wished to marry would be allowed to marry legally, or would have to settle for just living with one another. If the couple had a son who liked to work with wood, it was the slaveholder, not the child's parents who decided whether he would be trained as a carpenter, just as it was the slaveholder who gave or withheld permission for the parents to teach their daughter to read. It was the slaveholder, not the parents who decided whether their children would be baptized, or if they were baptized, whether they would be baptized in the faith of their parents or one chosen by their master. The slaveholder even decided whether the family would remain together because he could, and did, sell husband away from wife and children away from parents.

Slavery prevented black parents from passing on the fruits of their labor to their children. By law, all that the slaves produced belonged to their master and his children. Most American immigrants arrived in North America, worked hard, accumulated some property and then passed it on to their children. As slaves were nonpersons they could pass nothing on to their children save by permission of a slaveowner. He or she might permit the slave to pass on a musical instru-ment, a tool box, or a Bible, but no slaveholder had to allow even this and few let slaves pass on any substantive property to their children.

Because the slaves had no protection for their families, the property they produced, or even themselves they became the most watchful of America's many peoples. Defenseless before the law and with many Christian clerics arguing that God had cursed the descendants of Ham to forever serve whites, the slaves carefully watched white people and in this watchful reflectivity is to be found the origin of blackness. Their very survival depended not on an understanding of the law or of their rights as citizens—though many slaves were surprisingly knowledgeable of American rights—but on an accurate reading of white attitudes and intentions. Of course, all Americans had to be watchful as together they went about building a New World. Whether Native

American, Euro-American, or recent immigrant, the inhabitants watched and learned from one another. The earliest settlers learned from Indians, Indians adopted many of the material items of whites, and immigrants, with an eye on other Americans, adapted their own cultures in such a way as to retain some of the old and incorporate some of the new. The slaves were faced with the same environmental, social, and cultural problems as confronted all other Americans, but because they had far less control over their lives, they relied far more than other Americans on themselves and their intelligence and far less on institutions such as the law. It is therefore one of history's many ironies that slaves have been presented as mindless simpletons when in fact they were the most watchful and reflective of Americans.

Race, in the biological sense in which it is usually employed, had nothing to do with this watchful reflectivity. Those enslaved were sometimes mostly black, sometimes mostly white, sometimes mostly Indian, and at other times of such mixed ancestry that it was impossible to determine which racial group had contributed the most to the racial makeup of the slave. It was therefore not race that played the central role in shaping blackness, but slavery. All slaves were, or were believed to be, the descendants of Africans. Slaveholders and their supporters acknowledged that some of their living property might be of mixed ancestry, but the one drop rule rendered such biological realities socially meaningless. All persons of any known African ancestry were black, and only blacks were slaves. But just as this justification for slavery served slavemasters, so too did it serve the slaves, and hence African Americans, for blackness was rooted not in the idea of racial purity, but rather in the shared necessity, as slaves, of watching whites.

Because whites were in power, they had the luxury of treating all blacks as though they were the same. Indeed, it was in their ideological and material interest to behave as if blacks were identical in ability and according to Jones to create

public fiction to the effect that all Black people were inferior physically, intellectually, culturally, and morally to all white people. By public fiction, is meant here the collective, civic acceptance and promulgation of something individual members of the society know and privately concede to be untrue. Slaveholders, who pushed most strongly for the public fiction of Black inferiority, knew very well it was not true. As the works of Blassingame, Fogel and Engerman, Genovese, and Miller make clear, masters did not treat their slaves as if they were all the stupid, docile, immoral brutes they publicly proclaimed them to be. Instead, almost without exception, slaveowners drew careful distinctions among their slaves, recognizing which were intelligent, strong, rebellious, and which were not. To have operated a plantation as though all its resident bondsmen were the grinning simpletons of public fiction would have led to disaster. (1988:35)

White power gave whites the luxury of pretending that all blacks were inferior to all whites, just as it gave them the luxury of entering into relations with individual blacks which contradicted the public fiction of black inferiority.

Blacks had no such luxury and did not pretend that all whites were the same, so that blackness was therefore partly rooted in the necessary monitoring of whites. It was also partly rooted in the necessary monitoring of blacks. Africans in America and their American-born children watched one another as carefully as they watched whites and for the same reason. Slaves had no organized polity to discipline one another and to protect themselves from one another. Slave quarters were organized to serve the interests of the slaveholder and not the slaves. As a consequence, the slaves, unlike all other Americans, could neither publicly celebrate nor publicly discipline one another. Those who served the community at the expense of the master had to be covertly rewarded, just as those who served the master at the expense of the community had to be covertly punished.

Because the celebration of heroes and the punishment of villains had to be hidden from the slaveholder and supportive whites, the slave community was different from all other American communities in which public assemblies were held to see the war hero applauded or the murderer executed. This did not prevent the slaves from reaching a consensus as to how blacks ought to behave—a different way of saying they created blackness—nor did it prevent them from maintaining this consensus despite their enslavement. Webber writes:

Most [slave] quarter communities also generated and told stories which perpetuated the memory of more or less historical quarter figures. By building the legends of these persons through telling their story the quarter community gave great sanction to the deeds of these men and women. The legendary figures most often immortalized in story were of three general types: those who fooled or made fun of whites; those who sacrificed for family or friends; and those who physically confronted plantation authorities. (1978:21)

The slaves honored all three in their songs and tales, offering them as models for their children to emulate.

And emulate these heroic men and women they did, creating in the process one of the most remarkable societies in the annals of humankind. Without money, without property, without political power, without full control over their families, or even full control over their own bodies, American slaves created a society in which men and women delivered respect to one another. Perhaps even more remarkable, they did so in the shadows of the larger, more populous free white society, itself based on education, money, property, titles, and control over family life, all denied to slaves. Whites as free persons could behave in one way, blacks as slaves had to behave in another. Lacking freedom, black peoples created an alternative system, a means of respecting one another when the usual ways in which white Americans delivered respect were denied them. In deciding who deserved respect, European Americans looked at dress, education, occupation, degrees, size of residence, location of residence, number of servants employed, possessions, and titles. These were readily discerned at a glance so that a well-dressed merchant with a carriage and driver received more respect than a shabbily dressed workman who had neither. The difference in respect given the two men was supported by an emergent ideology which held that American society was an open one and the (presumably) hardworking merchant deserved respect, while the (presumably) lazy worker did not.

Their enslavement made it impossible for blacks to accept the ideology that Americans got what they deserved. They knew that they had done nothing to deserve slavery, and even if they had, their unborn children certainly did not deserve to be slaves. Blackness was rooted in the shrewd awareness of slaves that American society rested on lies. But beyond this awareness and more important was the fact that in the separate cultural world the slaves were creating they wore no obvious badges of respect. The slaves had few clothes, no titles, no degrees, no fine houses, and no servants. While whites ranked one another based on possessions and other obvious social markers, blacks ranked one another on the basis of behavior. Men and women in the slave quarters earned respect based on commitment to community, respect for the elderly, care for children, and belief in God. But, in sharp contrast to the white community, there were no easy markers, no quick way to determine at a glance that members of the slave community deserved respect. Only by means of watchfulness over a period of time could the slaves determine whether one of their fellows was good to his children, respected the elderly, was committed to the community, and believed in God.

Their very lives depended on the slaves watching and assessing one another. Most slave revolts in North America failed because they were betrayed. The slaves were placed in a cruel dilemma as the most successful revolt was the one with little planning, in which the rebels simply got up one morning and decided on rebellion. But although these revolts might succeed in the short run, they were destined to fail because the conspirators had not planned what to do after their initial success. Would-be rebels therefore devoted some time to planning, but ironically the more time they took in developing their plans, the more likely it was that the rebellion would be betrayed.

Whether they wished simply to maintain the slave community and continue delivering respect to one another, or whether they wished to rebel and overturn both this community and destroy the white community that governed it, the slaves watched one another. Just as the slaves never had the luxury of pretending all whites were the same, neither did they have the luxury of pretending all blacks were the same. In his overview of the 18th-century formation of African-American culture Kulikoff writes:

Even native-born slaves had little choice either about their work or about the people who lived with them in their quarters. Nevertheless, they had a small measure of self-determination in their family life, in their religion, and in the ways they celebrated and mourned. When they could choose, Afro-Americans simultaneously borrowed from whites and drew on the values and beliefs their ancestors brought from West Africa to form a culture not only significantly different from that of Anglo-Americans but also different from the culture of any West African group or any other group of North American slaves. (1986:346)

In the formation of this culture, and in maintaining it, the slaves had no alternative but to watch one another as carefully as they watched whites.

CONCLUSIONS

Blackness had its origin in the one drop rule, in the absence of ethnicity, and in slavery. Unlike whiteness, which is rooted in the belief that whites are racially pure and that being white is genetically determined, blackness makes no assumption that blacks are racially pure, nor that being black is genetically determined. Blacks and whites in the United States offer strikingly different explanations for behavior. Most white people, not all, really believe that race determines behavior and that when they see black people they know something of their physical capacities, intellectual limitations, and sexual inclinations. Whites come by this belief honestly enough, for their culture has taught them that blacks are an inferior, degraded people, strong, stupid, and oversexed. Most black people, not all, really believe that behavior is determined by choice, and that the choices made are moral ones. Blacks come by this belief honestly enough for their culture has taught them that some whites behave morally and others do not. The slaves distinguished among slavemasters, their supporters, abolitionists, and those whites who were neutral toward slavery. Today African Americans distinguish among whites who are racist, those who are antiracist, and those who claim—despite much evidence to the contrary—that racism is no longer a force in American society. Blacks draw these distinctions for the same reason as their slave ancestors, they do not have the luxury of pretending all whites are the same.

Blackness is behavioral, not genetic: it is based on choice, not race. This explains why race hate groups find so few followers among Afro-Americans. Many blacks hate whites, and they often turn out in large numbers to hear black demagogues who preach hatred of all whites, but most African Americans stop short of joining such groups. To do so would be to reject blackness by lumping all whites together. In the eyes of most blacks, this would mean making blackness just like whiteness and behaving just like whites who lump all blacks together. Blackness resembles whiteness in its acceptance of race as a conceptual category, but differs from it in that it argues neither for racial determinism nor for biological purity. Blackness resembles ethnicity in that it is culturally based, and in the context of American society it is not centered on economics or politics. Like most ethnic groups blacks have seldom sought to create independent polities or separate economies, although like most ethnic groups, blacks sometimes appeal to group solidarity as a means of accomplishing economic and political goals. Blackness differs from ethnicity in that it was created in North America and was not transported from Asia or

Europe. It also differs from ethnicity in that it was created by slaves, men and women who had far less control over their lives than did other Americans.

Blackness is not, however, fully independent of European-American ideas. Nowhere is this more clear than in the Afro-American color hierarchy. While the one drop rule prevented the development of the complex racial ranking of blacks, mulattos, quadroons, octoroons and other persons of color characteristic of Latin America and the Caribbean, it did not prevent many black Americans from accepting the idea that European physical features were beautiful and African ones ugly. In their opening paragraph on this color complex Russell, Wilson, and Hall (1992:1) observe: "Yet beneath a surface appearance of Black solidarity lies a matrix of attitudes about skin color and features in which color, *not character* [italics added] establishes friendships; degree of lightness, not expertise, influences hiring; and complexion, not talent, dictates casting for television and film." While blackness leads African Americans to focus on character, not on physical appearance, the cultural hegemony of whites leads them to accept the idea that a light-skinned spouse is preferable to a dark-skinned one. Physical appearance becomes more important than moral character. This color ranking is reversed when black Americans accept the white American stereotype that the darker the skin color, the more exciting the sex as reflected in the folk-saying, *The blacker the berry, the sweeter the juice.*

In addition to being influenced by Euro-American attitudes, blackness has come under attack in recent years. Biologists, geneticists, physical anthropologists, and other scientists deny that race is a valid biological construct. In general, they have demonstrated that white supremacy is based on the scientifically discredited idea that whites constitute a separate, distinct race, pure, isolated from, and superior to all other races. Similarly, the biracial/multiracial movement seeks to undercut ideas about white racial purity and thereby end racism, by insisting that its members are of mixed racial heritage (Jones 1994; Reddy 1994; Zack 1993). These two assaults on blackness share the assumption that blackness is the same as whiteness. The assumption is understandable as the one drop rule established the bipolar idea about race in which persons must be either black or white. The biracial movement has been especially aggressive in attacking blackness because many of its members assume that blacks have been the most resistant of all the nation's racial groups to the destruction of the bipolar idea about race. In this they are correct as biracialism has long been accepted by Asian Americans, Latinos, and Native Americans—where one may, for example, be part Asian and part white—but it strikes at and attacks the essence of blackness. It is not therefore surprising that many African Americans are hostile to the biracial movement. Ironically, the African–American community includes descendants of all racial groups, demanding of them only that they identify themselves as black and commit themselves to the struggle for racial justice as blacks.

There are two lessons in all this, one for nonblacks and the other for blacks. First, nonblacks must realize that blackness is not the same as whiteness. Although the two appear to be conceptually similar, and there are black preachers of race hate who mimic white racists, blackness and whiteness are different in their history and assumptions. Martin Luther King, Jr., looked forward to a time when people would be judged by the content of their character and not the color of their skin. In this he merely urged white Americans to behave like black Americans. Although blackness is not perfect, and although many black Americans accept the color hierarchy, other Americans might do well to emulate a culture that rewards those who love their children, respect the elderly, serve their community, and believe in God. Second, blacks must accept the idea that many persons who are phenotypically black do not wish to be black. Recent immigrants from Latin America and the Caribbean wish to hold on to their national identity, the grandchildren of Cape Verdean immigrants wish to maintain a sense of being Cape Verdean, and many new immigrants from Africa are committed to an African ethnicity. Some biracials of African ancestry want to separate themselves from the African-American community. While the majority of these persons appreciate the long African-American struggle for justice, most of them are committed to it, and some of them consider themselves as black, they do not want to see their sense of self submerged in blackness. The culture of blackness demands that African Americans allow these people not to be black. Just as the slaves allowed persons of mixed race ancestry to be black, so must their descendants allow persons of mixed race not to be black if this is their choice.

REFERENCES

Asante, M. K. 1988. *Afrocentricity*. Trenton, N.J.: Africa World Press.
Axtell, J. 1981. *The European and the Indian: Essays in the Ethnohistory of Colonial North America*. New York: Oxford University Press.
Bailyn, B. 1967. *The Ideological Origins of the American Revolution*. Cambridge, Mass.: Belknap Press.
Bateman, R. B. 1990. Africans and Indians: A Comparative Study of the Black Carib and Black Seminole. *Ethnohistory* 37: 1–24.
Bennett, L., Jr. 1970. The Road Not Taken. *Ebony* 51: 71–77.
Boateng, F. 1993. Institutionalized Sexism and the African American Male: Implications for Gender Relations. *The Afrocentric Scholar* 2:1–11.
Brace, C. L. 1995. Clines and Clusters versus Race in the Assessment of Human Variation. Paper presented at the Annual Meeting of the American Association for the Advancement of Science, Atlanta, February 20.
Collins, B. 1985. *White Society in the Antebellum South*. New York: Longman.
Davis, F. J. 1991.*Who Is Black? One Nation's Definition*. University Park: University of Pennsylvania Press.
Dowd, G. E. 1993. *A Spirited Resistance: The North American Indian Struggle for Unity, 1745–1815*. Baltimore: The Johns Hopkins University Press.
Flanders, R. 1933. *Plantation Slavery in Georgia*. Chapel Hill: University of North Carolina Press.
Fredrickson, G.M. 1981. *White Supremacy: A Comparative Study in American and South African History*. New York: Oxford University Press.

Herrnstein, R. J. and Murray, C. 1994. *The Bell Curve: Intelligence and Class Structure in America*. New York: Macmillan.

Herskovits, M. J. 1941. *The Myth of the Negro Past*. New York: Harper and Brothers.

Higginbotham, A. L., Jr. 1980. *In the Matter of Color—Race and the American Legal Process: The Colonial Period*. New York: Oxford University Press.

Horsman, R. 1981. *Race and Manifest Destiny: The Origins of American Racial Anglo-Saxonism*. Cambridge, Mass.: Harvard University Press.

Issac, R. 1982. *The Transformation of Virginia, 1740–1790*. Chapel Hill: University of North Carolina Press.

Jones, R.S. 1978. Structural Isolation, Race, and Cruelty in the New World. *Third World Review* 4: 34–43.

———. 1988. In the Absence of Ideology: Blacks in Colonial America and the Modern Black Experience. *The Western Journal of Black Studies* 12: 30–39.

———. 1994. The End of Africanity? The Bi-Racial Assault on Blackness. *Western Journal of Black Studies* 18: 201–211.

Jordan, W. D. 1968. *White over Black*. Chapel Hill: University of North Carolina Press.

Kaplan, S. 1973. *The Black Presence in the Era of the American Revolution, 1770–1800*. Greenwich, Conn.: New York Graphic Society.

Katz, S. H. 1995. The American Association of Physical Science Revised UNESCO Statement on Race: A Brief Analysis and Commentary. Paper presented at the Annual Meeting of the American Association for the Advancement of Science, Atlanta, February 20.

Koger, L. 1985. *Black Slaveowners: Free Black Slave Masters in South Carolina, 1790–1860*. Jefferson, N.C.: McFarland.

Kovel, J. 1970. *White Racism: A Psychohistory*. New York: Pantheon.

Kulikoff, A. 1986. *Tobacco and Slaves: The Development of Southern Cultures in the Chesapeake, 1680–1800*. Chapel Hill: University of North Carolina Press.

Littlefield, D. F., Jr. 1977. *Africans and Seminoles: From Removal to Emancipation*. Westport, Conn.: Greenwood Press.

McLoughlin, W.G. 1986. *Cherokee Renascence in the New Republic*. Princeton, N.J.: Princeton University Press.

McLoughlin, W.G., Conser, W.H. and McLoughlin, V.D. 1984. *The Cherokee Ghost Dance: Essays on the Southeastern Indians, 1789–1861*. Macon, Ga.: Mercer University Press.

McManus, E. J. 1973. *Black Bondage in the North*. Syracuse, N.Y.: Syracuse University Press.

Mellafe, R. 1975. *Negro Slavery in Latin America*. Translated by J.W.S. Judge. Berkeley: University of California Press.

Metraux, A. 1972. *Voodoo in Haiti*. Translated by Hugo Charteris. New York: Schocken Books.

Morgan, E. 1975. *American Slavery—American Freedom: The Ordeal of Colonial Virginia*. New York: W.W. Norton.

Morner, M. 1967. *Race Mixture in the History of Latin America*. Boston: Little, Brown.

Murphy, J. M. 1993. *Santeria: African Spirits in America*. Boston: Beacon Press.

Perdue, T. 1979. *Slavery and the Evolution of Cherokee Society, 1540–1866*. Knoxville: University of Tennessee Press.

Raboteau, A. J. 1980. *Slave Religion: The Invisible Institution in the Antebellum South*. New York: Oxford University Press.

Reddy, M. T. 1994. *Crossing the Color Line: Race, Parenting, and Culture*. New Brunswick, N.J.: Rutgers University Press.

Reuter, E. B. 1918. *The Mulatto in the United States*. Boston: Richard C.Badger.

Richter, D. K. 1992. "Some of Them Would Always Have a Minister with Them." Mohawk Protestantism, 1638–1719. *American Indian Quarterly* 16: 471–484.

Rout, L. B., Jr. 1976. *The African Experience in Spanish America*. New York: Cambridge University Press.

Russell, K., Wilson, M. and Hall, R. 1992. *The Color Complex: The Politics of Skin Color Among African Americans*. New York: Harcourt Brace Jovanovich.

Scarborough, R. 1933. *The Opposition to Slavery in Georgia Prior to 1860*. Nashville, Tenn.: George Peabody College for Teachers.

Sobel, M. 1987. *The World They Made Together: Black and White Values in Eighteenth Century Virginia*. Princeton, N.J.: Princeton University Press.

Stuckey, S. 1987. *Slave Culture: Nationalist Theory and the Foundations of Black America*. New York: Oxford University Press.

Thomas, G.E. 1975. Puritans, Indians and the Concept of Race. *New England Quarterly* 48:3–27.

Walker, D. 1965. *David Walker's Appeal*. New York: Hill and Wang. First published, 1829. (Page references are to the 1965 edition.)

Webber, T. L. 1978. *Deep Like the Rivers: Education in the Slave Quarter Community, 1831–1865*. New York: W.W. Norton.

Welsing, F. C. 1970. *The Cress Theory of Color-Confrontation and Racism*. Privately published.

Wood, G. S. 1992. *The Radicalism of the American Revolution*. New York: Alfred A. Knopf.

Woods, Sister F. J. 1972. *Marginality and Identity: A Colored Creole Family Through Ten Generations*. Baton Rouge: Louisiana State University Press.

Woodward, C. V. 1957. *The Strange Career of Jim Crow*. New York: Galaxy Book.

Zack, N. 1993. *Race and Mixed Race*. Philadelphia: Temple University Press.

CHAPTER 5

Visual Images of the Postcolonial Blues on the Corner of Toulouse and Royal: Discord and Identity in *Songs of My People*

Helán E. Page with D. France Olivieira

Songs of My People (1992) is a book of photographic images edited by Eric Easter, D. Michael Cheers, and Dudley M. Brooks, three African-American associates of New African Visions Incorporated.[1] This project was organized into a traveling museum exhibition that began its three-year national tour in January 1992. How should we read these images? What are their humanscapes trying to tell us about African America? What claims do they make about the identity, status, and well-being of black people in America today? In whose interest does the mass audience's resistance or receptivity to their embedded messages shift the balance of power in the relations of cultural production? In this chapter, Page ethnographically examines a set of black visual images and the relations of production that serve the nation by generating that imagery. Page also examines the mediated construction of black identity. Our focus is on how such organizations and their representatives behave when trying to intersect. We infer that the editor/organizers of *Songs of My People* wanted to succeed in their organizational endeavor and relied on their project to counter "negative" mainstream representations with images popularly deemed more "positive" about African Americans.

INTRODUCTION

While warranting acclaim for its aesthetic appeal, this exceedingly popular collection of black visual imagery (*Songs of My People*) is not only being circulated in book form, but also its editors sold corporate and federal sponsors the idea that this project should be organized into a traveling museum exhibition that began its three-year national tour in January of 1992.[2] We believe that anthropology is prepared to address questions adequately about the generation of cultural images, but not with the same old methods. Indeed, our usual suppositions about what constitutes good ethnographic research must be suspended. This ethnographic study is not the usual kind, and it is as much theoretical as applied. It is also another example of homework, somewhat different from that of Brackette Williams (1995). Whereas Williams appropriated anthropology's fieldwork strategies of participant-observation and brought them home in an appropriately modified fashion to study her role as a citizen and fellow passenger/driver in the modern practices of homeless begging and commuter giving, we developed another set of methods that helped us look at yet another aspect of modern life in Western society—the mediated construction of *black identity*.

In this chapter, we ethnographically examine a set of black visual images and the relations of production which serve the nation by generating that imagery. Like Williams, we too assume the role of citizen observers too, but we interrogate the behavior of a few fellow citizens only where they participate in the relations of production that gave life to *Songs of My People*. We set out both to question and explain why this set of imagery, was so well received. Specifically, we develop a critique of *Songs of My People* as a particular set of black visual imagery and we treat this collection as a material product of modern visual representation practices adopted by African-American visual entrepreneurs who sought to project a successful black identity and who won the sponsorship of federal agents of museum administration and corporate managerial elites.

Our focus is less on the internal dynamics of organizations themselves than on how such organizations and their representatives behave when trying to produce a successful project in the crucible of complex social interactions where dominance and subordinance intersect. Many things occur at that intersection—between the construction of racialized identity, the daily reproduction of racism as a system of resource stratification, and the active consumption of information in the form of black visual imagery. When we examine *Songs of My People,* we observe African-American visual entrepreneurs attempting to counter the "negative" black imagery typically promoted by the mainstream media with "positive" black imagery. Unfortunately, they reproduce mainstream categories in ways that ultimately enhance the relations of domination that make black acts of cultural production into objects of commodification and subject black self-representations to greater dominant group control. We do not contextualize our analysis simply as an aesthetic critique of the photographs, or the photographers, instead, we seek to understand how three subaltern visual entrepreneurs implemented an image-selection process that narrowed their audiences' potential view of black life in the United States. We hypothesize that the selected images legitimate a discourse which claims that African Americans, generally, have overcome the barriers of racism and have "made it" in the United States. Meanwhile, a subjugated, subaltern discourse about African America's crisis is acknowledged only superficially by editor/organizers who apparently tried to circumvent rather than confront it.

Yet, we argue that their choices made this project both safe and successful as opposed to most projects attempted by visual activists who are more often denied success and broad access to mass audiences. This is partly because visual activists persistently confront those who are most protected or privileged by mainstream safety. By questioning mainstream categories and by highlighting the distasteful features of America's diversity politics, visual activists conscientiously attempt to liberate the hold of those categories on our mass mind. In contrast, the editor/organizers of *Songs of My People* produced images that constitute a mainstream representation of African American life to the exclusion of African America's full range of diversity. By means of the imagery organized by these three African-American visual entrepreneurs, black life in the United States is discursively "mainstreamed" in a way that tends to consolidate a location in white public space[3] where white America continues to feel safe and where African America is, momentarily, allowed to feel proud.

Sally Falk Moore (1987:730) advised anthropologists to identify and describe diagnostic events that expose "ongoing contests and conflicts and competitions and the efforts to prevent, suppress, or repress these." She challenged us to discover "the place of the small-scale event in the large-scale historical process" (1987:730) and to reveal "the extent to which the manufacture and control of particular cultural and social constructions is or is not in local hands" (Moore 1987:736). Frederick Barth (1989:130) echoed a similar view when he explained that "People participate in multiple, more or less discrepant, universes of discourse; they construct different, partial and simultaneous worlds in which they move; their cultural construction of reality springs not from one source and is not of one piece." Like Moore, Barth urged us to detect where meanings are generated in the social order and to ask how those meanings—and the symbolic products conveying them—actually serve to identify processes of cultural production with the concept of authorship (1989:133).

The photographs, the book, and the traveling exhibits are all material artifacts of visual representation activity. We insist that the relations of production that made and distribute these objects can be ethnographically observed without ethnographers having to be present at the organizational sites where such interactions and exchanges take place. In fact, such interactions and exchanges would normally be hidden from us and many anthropologists have used this fact as one reason why ethnographic research in the United States is too hard to do. Even with permission to observe simultaneously all the actors as they dialogically conceived, negotiated, planned, and implemented this project from within each organization, the multiple interactions taking place at each site where we could assign an observer would be dramatically altered—both by the presence of our research team and by our permission to be present.

Thus, we attempt to trace the production of the material artifacts in a way similar to Sidney Mintz's ethnography of the rise of sugar markets and sugar consumption. Whereas Mintz covered centuries, our study covers only a few months at its core and about ten years at its widest point of extension. Yet, this is not a longitudinal study. It focuses on the present moment of a contemporary event. The social behavior involved is encoded in the energetic breath that organized the human action that gave life and birth to this project. That breath, at the point of its inspiration and expiration, can be observed ethnographically through an analysis which, following Barth (1989) begins by recognizing (1) that meaning lies in the dialogical relationship between social actors, (2) that culture is not always homogeneously shared but its distributed, nonshared aspects can be analyzed, (3) that subjects are always positioned, with no position having "privileged validity," and (4) that events diverge from actual, presumed, or alleged intent because they are dialectical products of social interaction and material forces. The same criteria guide the present inquiry.

A corollary of our hypothesis is that these images encode a "strategic contestation" that Stuart Hall (1992:26) believes has always been underway. In his view, the everyday experiences of African Americans always have been strategically rendered into popular representations and thus, have always been available for expropriation (Hall 1992:26). On one hand, we inquire into the politics of representation reflected in them. On the other hand, our critique of the representational practices that selected, organized, and interpreted these images for their mass audience avoids claiming or disclaiming their accuracy. Instead of falling into the essentialist trap of trying to assess the accuracy of the selected images, we are satisfied to explain their mass appeal and to outline the parameters of that appeal which delineate the parameters of acceptable African-American diversity in the nation. We simply expose the popular desires and fantasies exhibited in the "profoundly mythic" quality of this very appealing black imagery (Hall 1992:32).

As scholars of anthropology, we assume an activist stance and forgo the advantages that might accrue if we took a more entrepreneurial attitude towards this work. It is not widely deemed professional to advocate on behalf of the groups that we anthropologists study, especially if the group studied is your own group of origin. However, we are convinced that African Americans, and others who become spectators of these images, would be better equipped as active, not passive, consumers who are seeking out these images and who must ultimately interpret them if activist anthropologists are to share their expertise with fellow citizens (who may never go to school or attend college). Anthropological activism can demonstrate its value as an applied behavioral science by helping the mass audience be aware of three important points related to their interpretation of *Songs of My People*, but the effects of that expanded awareness would not be limited to that project.

First, people may more effectively struggle for greater local control over their own acts of cultural production whether they are displayed in their community, in the media, or in the museum. We can assist their efforts to understand the implications of their struggles over racial identity by helping them find the language to voice what they already know—that such struggles are always negotiated between dominant and subordinate positions in audiovisual imagery produced for mass consumption (Hall 1992:28). Second, people can be encouraged to recognize and face the fact that portrayals of black life in the

United States by African Americans are always going to reflect how we are both African and American (Gilroy 1993; Hall 1992:29; Wallace 1990:45–46).[4] Third, people who are anthropologically trained to be cognizant of their location between the production of black visual imagery and the shifting parameters of African America's hybrid identity will come to realize and proclaim (in their own language and not in the language of our scholarly discourse) that all their group's adaptive flexibility is put at risk when so much of its diversity is subjected to the

> scene, par excellence, of commodification, of the industries where culture enters directly into the circuits of a dominant technology—the circuits of power and capital. It is the space of homogenization where stereotyping and the formulaic mercilessly process the material and experiences it draws into its web, where control over narratives and representations passes into the hands of the established cultural bureaucracies. (Hall 1992:26)

We demonstrate that in the "circuits of power and capital" incredible contradictions can occur. Illustratively, the images in *Songs of My People* were compiled by three male members of the black subordinate group, yet the same images contain homogenizing or "whitening" categories that may be read as mainstream representations of black life in America. We argue that the three editor/organizers, however inadvertently, visually represent black identities as being "whitened" so as to circumscribe a homogenizing comfort zone in which African America can feel pride in its experiential similarity with mainstream European America instead of shame in allegations of its pathological difference. That comfort zone is also a space in which mainstream European America can feel safe with its ominous perception of a national black presence. When viewed this way, as a specific product of black popular culture, *Songs of My People* becomes one site of cultural struggle "where we [African Americans] are imagined, where we are represented, not only to the audiences out there who [do or do not get the message], but to ourselves [as if] for the first time" (Hall 1992:28). How we choose to intervene in capitalist relations of production by representing ourselves to ourselves in a "positive" way can be problematic or liberating, depending on whether we behave like visual activists or take the path of least resistance when we choose to behave, in a organizationally successful manner, as visual entrepreneurs.

THE VISUAL ACTIVISTS' MODE OF CULTURAL PRODUCTION

Anthropologists often errantly presume that mainstream representations stand, necessarily, in opposition to the counter-representations generated by African Americans, Native Americans, Chicano Americans, Asian Americans, or Pacific Americans. We also recognize that anthropologists sometimes overlook the explanatory fact that upwardly mobile members of oppressed groups may, under certain conditions, elect to ratify "positive" mainstream representations of their own groups in their zeal to overcome the downward pull of "negative" mainstream representations of the past.

We believe that the editor/organizers of *Songs of My People* wanted to succeed in their organizational endeavor and relied on their project to counter "negative" mainstream representations with images popularly deemed more "positive." Their organizational stance in a cultural struggle which decides who gets to represent what images to which audiences is confrontational. They sought the approval and support of established organizational authority, which was more successful and fiscally powerful than their own. Thus, they do not confront the image-containing influence of those established organizations as former Harvard Law professor, Derrick Bell (1994), suggests that we must. Rather, they lay claim to the security and success that would be bestowed on them by such established organizations if the visual entrepreneurs created the kind of black imagery that could be safely contained within "the system." Consequently, their image-making work contrasts sharply with that of visual activists who confront and try to correct the "system," enactments that keep them locked out of its intimate embrace.

Among oppressed groups in the United States, some individuals operate on the margins of established organizations. They commit themselves to alternative modes of representation and they engage in oppositional visual media practices. Such visual activists seek to produce and distribute intimate images of their own group as well as interpretative images of the historic or contemporary relationship among dominant groups and between those groups and dominating mainstream America. Despite their unavoidable reliance on hybrid identities, visual activists inscribe meanings and identities in opposition to mainstream interpretations and modes of identity formation so as to confront and expose dominating practices. As Gerald Sider (1994:114) poignantly argues, typically, such activists are prone "both to create and at times also defy" their group's sense of collective history and identity.

As visual activists share, both with their group and with the dominant culture, salient understandings may be required to speak oppositionally. They share with the dominant group ideas such as, "Black people are not supposed to be proud," or "Indians are not supposed to have power," but the same visual activists may go on, as Sider (1994) explains, both to confront and to deny the constraining intent of these dominant representations. They might do that, says Sider, by creating a tee shirt or a more formal piece of art that assertively proclaims "Black and Proud," or "Red Power." Embodying group-affirmative ideas, activist art is deemed unrefined and low-culture, because it is broadcasting a message that overtly contests mainstream America's right to dominate, and in turn, mainstream America finds such messages repugnant, not because they are false, but because they might be recognized as true. If taken as true, such messages threaten to shift the status quo relations that makes mainstream America feel safe. What is rejected, in the interest of safety, is not the whole group or even the minority artists themselves, but the unsafe oppositional message that threatens white public space with exposure. Representations of the same minority group by the same minority artist may be kept in a project, but only if that artist can be made to concede to a reorganization or reinterpretation of the visual imagery that he or she produced in a way that defends white public space and makes mainstream America feel safe. In that same space, African America is made/allowed to feel pride.

According to Masilela (1993) one incidence of such a cultural struggle involved Charles Burnett and a private funding agency. Burnett wished to make a documentary film about recent immigrants to America that would remain true to the representational and interpretive visual "traditions" that he previously had established as an independent black filmmaker. As a noted visual activist who had earned a mainstream reputation by making independent black films, Burnett wanted the freedom to presume that the First Amendment right to "freedom of speech" would preserve his representational and interpretive control over the film if he decided to seek private funds and sponsorship.

In good faith, Burnett shot his film and named it after Langston Hughes's poem, *America Becoming*. In the film Burnett tried to portray the discordance that emerges among Asian, Latin American, African American and Caribbean immigrant groups as they attempt to assimilate into America. Whereas Burnett sought to highlight the conflictual and crisis-ridden experiences of immigrant groups, Masilela (1993:113) reports that the Ford Foundation, which sponsored the film, "imposed a harmonious interpretation." Burnett complained about the foundation's interpretive interference while shooting the film, and it was also noted in Henry Chu's review of *America Becoming* in the *Los Angeles Times* (Masilela 1993:117n).

Based on prior experience, Burnett feared that trying to interpret immigration to a mainstream American audience from a critical black perspective would most likely be blocked by the white (and maybe even black) media agents, sponsors, or publicists who usually govern access to the productive means of representation. Even when Burnett managed to circumvent such obstacles, his film was controlled through channels of distribution. Although his film, *To Sleep with Anger* (focusing on struggles with closeness and identity among an African-American family who migrated to Los Angeles from the rural South), won awards for its screenplay from the Independent Spirit Awards and from the National Society of Film Critics, its circulation and marketing were so tightly controlled that it was shown mainly to all-white audiences (Masilela 1993: 117n).

Visual activists like Burnett struggle to escape the dominant interpretations that are so often imposed in Hollywood and at other sites of mainstream imagery control. They not only deny the dominant culture's interpretation of shared situations or events, but they also confront such interpretations head-on in an effort to subvert them. Visual activists of this caliber also understand that their subversive efforts can quickly evoke mainstream retaliation or retribution. Even if they want to be recognized as truly professional artists, or be rewarded for their labor with success and material security, visual activists rarely expect to achieve those amenities as long as the oppositional nature of their activism keeps calling dominant mainstream representational categories into question.

Since visual activists typically provide mass audiences with oppositional alternatives to mainstream interpretive imagery, they are often relegated, as Halleck and Magnan (1993:156) explain, to domains "outside the power of mainstream media." Even from marginal locations, where visual activists like Burnett are denied supportive access to the means of representation, their image-making tactics defy regulation and voice the concerns of disenfranchised communities. Not only might they work, like Trihn T. Minha, Marlon Riggs, or Gloria Anzaldua (Behar 1993), on behalf of people whose racial and gender identities fall outside the European-American mainstream, but also they work just as hard to expose the impact of domination on all marginalized communities in which the subjects of their imagery live their lives. For these reasons, the imagery constructed by visual activists is often deemed unsafe by mainstream critics. Thus, their work must be contrasted with the successful and safer work of the visual entrepreneurs who organized the imagery in *Songs of My People*.

THE MUTED VOICE AS VISUAL ENTREPRENEUR

When Halleck and Magnan (1993) essentialize the idea of activist media being made by and for "others," they confuse the problem and make it difficult to analyze *Songs of My People*. For them, the "others" who create activist media images of and for their own group include "those who traditionally have not had [a] speaking voice in Western culture, except when mediated by "experts." Yet, the editor/organizers of *Songs of My People* easily fall into that category, and that is precisely why their project is regarded as such an accomplishment. They were silenced yet they spoke.

In the past, African Americans have had little access that would enable them to voice a "positive" image of African-American life. As an instructive example, Wallace (1990:47) reminds us that "the absence of black voices in the debate over the Primitivism show at the Museum of Modern Art in 1984 was no accident." The black artistic voice is normally silenced in museums that typically hang high-culture art, she argues, because most administrators and curators regard the modernism extolled by such museums as "the culmination of universal aesthetic values and standards." Wallace goes on to suggest that curators shifted their audiences' visual gaze from a celebration of Modernism onto an unusual exhibition of Primitivism. This represents the curator's power to shift the audiences' attention away from the habitual intentional object of Western aesthetics and toward the culturally different intentional object of Western anthropology, which has, in the past, regarded itself, as an organized discipline, the guardian of a primitive world "in need of preservation" and fundamentally "incapable of describing itself."

Furthermore, Wallace (1990) continues, the curator is armed with the anthropological notion of cultural relativism that allows him or her to persuade unconvinced colleagues to recognize that these "primitive" artists are also human. At that point, it soon starts to make sense to those fellow curators that "so called primitive art would be as good as Western art" and would thus merit exhibition. To sum up her point, Wallace (1990:47) deftly cites James Clifford who challenged professional anthropology to reassess our museumology when he said, "The fact that rather abruptly, in the space of a few decades, a large class of non-Western artifacts came to be redefined as art is a taxonomic shift that requires critical historical discussion, not celebration."

If we imagine that some people still regard African Americans as modernized primitives who reside as an internal colony of a racial colonial state, then it is not such a leap to imagine our artistic expression as another kind of primitivism that many curators believe should be on display. Low-culture visual activist art is not typically displayed in the finest museums, but images professionally organized by visual entrepreneurs like New African Visions Incorporated easily might be.[5]

Instead of including any activist imagery that might call mainstream representational categories into question, the editor/organizers tacitly countered "negative" mainstream attributions by safely affirming African America's "positive" mainstream attributions. This representational tactic was bound to be successful, and successful it was! It allowed the associates of New African Visions Incorporated to *clean up* African America's public image while allowing white, middle-class, and elite elements of the mainstream audience to feel completely safe with this calculated and controlled image correction.

The organizational base of the visual entrepreneur gives him or her the competitive edge over the visual activist. That is not simply because the entrepreneur is organized and the activist is not; rather, it is more because the networks of association affiliated with the entrepreneur require a degree of homogenization and conformity that the activist finds corrosive of their interpretive mode and antithetical to their oppositional message. An additional factor is that African-American audiences are more likely to hear about and seek out the visual entrepreneur's widely advertised and promoted work and may never hear about that of the activist. Or the entrepreneur's exhibit is likely to be in a more accessible place for an accessible length of time, whereas the work of the activist is more likely to be in an obscure place for a brief duration that does not accommodate a working-class daily schedule. Moreover, after centuries of consuming widely distributed public stereotypes of itself, the African-American mass audience has been conditioned to react with shame and to reject any black imagery it deems "negative" and to hungrily consume "positive" black imagery that enables a sensation of pride. Consequently, *Songs of My People* is widely sanctioned by African-American audiences, not because it is necessarily an accurate representation of their collective experience, but mainly because it serves as a balm for wounds to their collective self-esteem inflicted by "negative" black imagery.

Since "positive" imagery obviously seems better than "negative" imagery, African America embraced *Songs of My People* uncritically, with a sigh of relief. In that moment of their felicity, few who have witnessed this imagery have not been seduced by it, and fewer still have been willing or able to ask if our reactive embrace of this positive black imagery poses any problems for our collective identity formation process as African-American people. Must our diverse identities necessarily translate into a rhetoric of black essentials characterized by the divergent pragmatics of collective disunity? Or, in our thirst for a positive black image, are we willingly agreeing to homogenize the imagery of our own group so as to squeeze out embarrassing diversities that uncomfortably fail to measure up to mainstream behavioral standards? And if we refuse to do that, or fail to permit that squeezing to occur or fail to promote it, then what price do we pay?

In conclusion, there can be no strict dichotomy distinguishing visual activists from visual entrepreneurs. Similarly, there is no essentialist divide between negative and positive imagery. While activists and entrepreneurs may sometimes agree on what constitutes negative and positive visual imagery, more often than not, each is quite likely to regard key elements of the other's preferred imagery as fundamentally negative. In other words, they compete over how they, as black image-makers, will represent African America to itself.

PAYING THE COST OF UNFAVORABLE MAINSTREAM JUDGMENT

We offer a critique of the dominant narrative governing the regulated visibility of African-American bodies in *Songs of My People*, but our offer risks offending media agents, museum administrators, corporate managers, and any scholars who guard the citadels of representational control. Even to question the black imagery in a popular collection like *Songs of My People* is to violate mainstream sensibilities. Nevertheless, we question the extent to which a "positive" mainstream view of African-American life has been privileged in *Songs of My People*. Does that privileged portrayal obscure the full range of African-American diversity? Stuart Hall (1992) shares our concern that diverse black identities should be represented rather than monolithically essentialized into one best, right, or proper identity. He defends all our differences and is very quick to

acknowledge that the spaces "won" for difference are few and far between, that they are very carefully policed and regulated. I know, to my cost, that they are grossly underfunded, that there is always a price of incorporation to be paid when the cutting edge of difference and transgression is blunted into spectacularization. I know that what replaces invisibility is a kind of carefully regulated, segregated visibility. (Hall 1992:24)

Halleck and Magnan (1993:154) verified the existence of such a regulatory cost when they found media agents responding "nastily" to a museum exhibit that they deemed appropriate:

When "non-professionals" point their cameras beyond the confines of family pictures, hackles are raised. This is true for ethnographic media making and art exhibition. Women and "multicultural" artists can be safely curated into programs about the family, the body or ethnic identity, but if the work takes a larger perspective, the uproar starts. The work is branded as "political," "agitprop" and lacking in aesthetic qualities.

Most images in *Songs of My People* escape the maligning impact of such an authorized dismissal, but the Whitney Biennial exhibition did not escape. Because its organizers dared to display the oppositional imagery of visual activists, that exhibit symbolically challenged mainstream assumptions about life in America, and so, it was maligned. This should come as no surprise. Many mainstream media agents react hysterically when confronted with activist subaltern imagery. Fueled by their almost constant exposure to educational myths, commercial television, and box-office films, mainstream media agents have constructed in their heads a status quo picture of race, class and gender relations that make them feel safe. In this picture, the domain of art is usually kept conceptually separate and distinct from the domain of the political. Any exhibited imagery that questions the picture in their heads will be read as a case exemplifying the wrongful politicization of art and may incite their irritation.

The outcries in the mainstream press over the politicization of contemporary art at the Whitney Biennial of 1993 provides the example of the month. In this case, an exhibit marked by its inclusion of "other" artists (in which even the amateur video of Rodney King's beating is screened) is branded [by mainstream media agents as] "Killed by Good Intentions," "Fade From White," "A Showcase of Political Correctness." (Halleck and Magnan 1993:154)

According to Halleck and Magnan (1993:16n), one media agent who worked for the *Los Angeles Times* suggested that the organizers of the Whitney Biennial "killed" their own exhibition with "good intentions" that errantly led them to liberally embrace diversity and inclusivity. Peter Plagens of *Newsweek* commented on the organizers' attempt to give "center stage to women, gays and artists of color" as evidence of their disorientation, as "fading" from the "white" mainstream view of American life. *Wall Street Journal* critic, Deborah Solomon, denounced the "political correctness" she imputed to the Whitney Biennial and pejoratively portrayed it as "the most disturbing museum show in living memory."

Following this scathing media barrage, certain costs or penalties may be imposed on some exhibit organizers. It may become difficult for some of them to find funding for future exhibitions of a similar nature. Some may not be promoted for a time after risking such exposure and having suffered public reprimand. Or, someone may be required to take a "fall," like the Jewish corporate executive, Mr. Enright, in Robert Redford's *Quiz Show* (1994). Yet, when they first decided to democratize museum exhibitions, we wonder if any of those organizers realized that they were taking such a risk. If their private, federal, or corporate sponsors agreed to support a project that they thought would result in a mainstream "treatment" of [primitive] minority art, then all the organizers risked professional and economic security when they allowed poignant "untreated" oppositional perspectives to be so prominently displayed.

Given that the unreceptive comments of those highly critical media agents had a tactical thrust, and given the reputation of those publications for which they write, the emotional quality of their widely publicized dismissive responses to the Whitney Biennial broadly imposed an exclusionary sanction. Furthermore, such a sanction serves to discourage the would-be organizers of similar projects. We might conclude that when such sanctions are widely publicized in reputable venues, an enclosure of white public space happens which squeezes out any threatening products, producers, and artists of a visual activist type while invalidating them as unworthy of mainstream funding or audience support.

Such a case demonstrates that Hall (1992) was not merely speculating about the price to be paid for visible incorporation into the spectacularization process known as exhibitions. When subaltern "others" are incorporated into regulated visibility, and out of the shadows of our prior invisibility, we are all expected, in return, to be interpretively aligned with mainstream conceptions of white public space, without overtly appearing to do so. We are even expected to pretend that white public space is like the pink elephant that does not exist. We are expected to affirm that all public space is democratized and that its racial allocation is no longer an issue since the civil rights movement. In the alternative, any divergence on our part from mainstream interpretive expectations can, and often will, evoke denunciative responses. At worst, exclusionary sanction can ostracize or bankrupt us; at best, it may mark us as "provocative" and render us subject to surveillance.

The simple lesson, in many instances, is that an inhibitive cost is exacted by established organizations that own the power of exclusionary sanction against any visual activists who dare to threaten the conceptual boundaries of white public space and the barriers of mainstream safety by promoting any oppositional representations of mainstream life in America. Visual activists who insist on this path risk their career and ignore clues which suggest that an inhibiting cost signals an inviolable but unspoken prohibition. In contrast, visual entrepreneurs learn to steer clear of that unstated prohibition, as if it were protected by a razor-wire barrier, once they come to understand that success, and indeed, their very professional survival, is predicated on its respectful observation.

A VISUAL ASSESSMENT OF REGULATED VISIBILITY

In contrast to the Whitney Biennial, *Songs of My People* won mainstream acclaim. With ample support from the Time/Warner Corporation, and with film donated by the Kodak Corporation, the organizers did not hire a cadre of visual activists who might submit oppositional black imagery. Instead, they report having carefully hired fifty "professional" African-American photographers. In other words, they selected against visual activists whose access to professional status is normally blocked, and selected in favor of fifty "professional" photographers on whom they could rely to help them safely achieve mainstream success.

In Addition, the images selected for inclusion would have to have mainstream appeal and would have to avoid inciting mainstream ire. Not only was the size of the book and its exhibitions another explicit constraint,[6] but as we show in the following discussions, a subtle and disavowed implicit effort was made to achieve a mode of visual coherency that would regulate African-American imagery by containing it within mainstream parameters. Because of these explicit and implicit organizational constraints, the project was rendered a safe venture, both for the African-American professionals associated with New African Visions Incorporated, and for their corporate and federal sponsors.

Nevertheless, the editor/organizers saw themselves countering a history of denigrating publicized black visual imagery[7] explored in films like *Ethnic Notions* and *Color Adjustment*, both by Marion Riggs. The City Museum of New York made a safe bet when its administration decided to support this project and was shocked by its popular appeal when the *Songs of My People* exhibit was there between September 23, 1992 and January 3, 1993. The American public hungrily responded with a fresh and resounding, "YES!" As measured by attendance, curators reported that the exhibition drew the largest audience in the museum's sixty-five-year history.[8] Other city museums across the nation have drawn similar numbers, but an unprecedented rate of attendance tells us more about reactions against "negative" black imagery than about the mass audience's uncritical concession to mediated "positive" black imagery.

To unveil this project's regulated form of black visibility, we must carefully examine the image-selection process. We evaluate those images with observational skills that most exhibition viewers or book perusers have never been taught. Out of 55,000 photographs shot across the nation, only 214 images were selected for the book and from those, only 152 were selected as feeders for the various exhibitions, tailored to reflect the local popular culture of each city along the national tour route. For the international tour, only 55 images were selected from among the 152.[9] The small number of images sent overseas calls attention to our concern about the range of possible interpretation being utterly constrained by a highly inflexible selection process.

We find it problematic that the selection criteria were never made available to the public. If consumers see only 55, or 152, or 214 of the total number of images shot, then on what grounds were 54,800 images of African-American life not selected? No answer is offered to publics who would have no reason to raise such a question if none of them realized that thousands of images had been rejected in favor of a few carefully chosen ones. This small range of representation narrows even more the range of acceptable interpretations concerning what is real, what is good, or what is possible or impossible in African-American life (Therborn 1985). This leads us to ask, What definitive messages are conveyed about African-American life, and how can we get at those messages?

Our methods for studying these images were governed by three issues that Sider (1994:109, 114-115) believes are at stake when struggles against oppression are rooted not merely in class-based confrontations, but also in what anthropologists once thought of as the object, culture, but increasingly understand as the process of cultural production. First, the images blur or omit certain forms of African-American identity while asserting as more worthy of attention the preferred forms of black identity. Second, they attest to the editor/organizers' effort to tacitly deny or distract attention from unpreferred features of African-American identity. Last, we embrace Sider's assertion that our anthropological notions of a European or African-American culture must be displaced by a deeper understanding of highly contested struggles—between various groups and within them—over how their shared experience should be reproduced and how different forms of group participation are to be represented. These criteria helped us to assess how different aspects of African America are made visible and invisible in this project.

Page's cursory review in 1993 initiated an analysis that only deepened as we started digging for the visually encoded meanings, which were less apparent at the surface level of conscious observations. We embarked on an archaeology of knowledge encoded in the images. We tried to uncover the categorical syntax of implicit visual meaning that we interpreted through our own everyday, educated, African-American visual repertoire. To meaningfully clump the image-instances we observed, we relied on in-group criteria of category inclusion, or exclusion which we believe are equally comprehensible to our own families and friends. We also presumed that most mainstream Americans may or may not have access to the same criteria, but we did not presume them to be necessarily unique to African-American experiences.

Initially, we listed the photographs and tallied them. Next, we examined each photograph for quantifiable image-instances that we construed as particular kinds of images constructed by the inescapable correspondence between the section of real-life referents and their photographic representation. We presumed that one photograph could have one, two, or more image-instances. For example, one photograph could contain two image-instances representing women and occupation. Another photograph could have three image-instances, representing men, leisure, and success. After scanning 203 pages of the book's visual text, we identified and typed 645 image instances.[10] That first scan confirmed our suspicion that image-instances are displayed in select but, implicit representational categories. We also wondered whether more select categorical distinctions might be revealed if we narrowed our inquiry down to the categories that seemed most salient for us (N=367) (Table 5.1).

Table 5.1
Major Category Values of Salient African American Image-Instances (N=367)

Image-Instance	No.	Image-Instance	No.
Elderly		*Spirituality*	
Active	29	Christian	14
Inactive	2	Islamic	3
Total	31 (8%)	African	5
Occupation		**Total**	22 (6%)
Independent	32	*Relational*	
White Collar	23	Family	32
Blue Collar	9	Friends	13
Laborer	15	Lovers	4
Unemployed	2	Colleagues	2
Total	81(22%)	Clients	13
Recreational		Constituency	3
Cheap Fun	26	**Total**	67(18%)
Costly Fun	5	*Town and Country*	
Work	31	Rural	22
School	12	Urban	43
Total	74(20%)	**Total**	65(18%)
Schooling		*Violence*	
Studying	2	Gang	1
Classroom	3	Drugs	1
Total	5(1%)	Police	1
Destitution		Prison	4
Homeless	4	Military	4
Street Performers	4	**Total**	11(3%)
Locations	4		
At Home	4		
Total	16 (4%)		
Category Totals=367			

We do not claim that most African Americans would necessarily organize the image instances as we do, nor do we presume that of any anthropologists who do visual work. Instead, we suggest that our categorizations reflect our own marginal vantage point as "minority" academics. The positioning of our marginality as blacks and as scholars in our racial society produces, for us, an analytical perspective that stands decidedly outside of mainstream modes of interpretation, both within the academy and outside of it. Thus, in this chapter we offer another plausible interpretation of *Songs of My People* that raises critical questions about the received interpretations of the mass audiences who are viewing it and of the mainstream media agents who acclaimed its success.

By focusing on this subset of the data, we instantly identified ascriptive trends. We could see, for example, that the editor/organizers selected images that fell into specific African-American categories as determined by a mainstream viewpoint. We found evidence of cultural struggle and a constrained portrayal of African-American diversity. We backed up our analysis through our own interpretations of project personnel behavior gleaned from press releases and from interviews conducted with one of the three project organizers who put us in telephone contact with several photographers who photographed for the project.

To avoid misquoting any of these professionals based only on notes taken on the computer during unstructured long-distance telephone interviews that were not taped, we quote none of them, but their comments did shape and add credibility to our argument. In the final analysis, we are prompted to argue that *Songs of My People* is visually constructed by an image-selection process, governed mainly by the organizers' adherence to mainstream standards of black social progress. Representational tactics and the intent of the visual entrepreneur predominate, and those of the visual activist, which might have made racialized mass audiences feel too unsafe or too ashamed, were avoided. The tactics employed stress how well African America has adopted mainstream standards of behavior. The inclusion of a few troubling black images is framed as an honest acknowledgment of a few unfortunate real-life exceptions to this general rule.

IT'S A HOPEFUL JAZZ THANG

The editor/organizers sought to counteract "five deadly ways" in which African Americans have been negatively represented in the media: that is, as "less intelligent, less hardworking, more violent, less universal, and less patriotic."[11] Images chosen to counter such themes do not necessarily constitute a self-portrait of African America, as they claim, but they quietly do insist that African Americans are different, though not "other." That is, the images suggest that blacks are human and fully American. At the same time, the editor/organizers disclaim any effort to tell a coherent story. "We set out not to create a symphony note for note, but a jazz conversation leaving each artist enough room to improvise and to capture what he or she felt" (Easter et al. 1992:ix).[12]

We consider it important to think about their assertions of black counteridentity and to summarize the actual storytelling contained in their images, disavowed by resorting to a jazz motif. To wit, a number of questions arise. For example, What new African visions of black life in America do the editor/organizers propose that federal and corporate sponsors found profitable to promote in the New World Order? Why did they prefer to organize the images in a *jazz* motif and reject the inescapable coherency of black spiritual, gospel, or blues organizational formats? Perhaps they used the term *jazz* in its individualistic sense, to rationalize the coherency imposed by the selection criteria on which they relied?[13] If the usage of the term *jazz* helped to deny a coherent story, then it also enabled them, at the same time, to deemphasize African America's discord while monolithically emphasizing "black beauty, achievements, diversity, African heritage and American-ness." That the organizers uncritically "treat" this particular set of themes and try to counteract the "five deadly ways" in which African Americans have been represented in the media suggests that they tell some story and achieved more coherency than they were willing to concede.

We believe that the United States Information Agency (USIA) relied on the international exhibition of *Songs of My People* to project a favorable image of the nation overseas.[14] The few images selected for international public consumption suggested that African Americans have progressed since the civil rights era and are finally starting to adapt to American society despite the bad news exaggerated by politically correct media agents. Perhaps in response to the conservative political climate, the organizers did not recklessly depict an economically desperate, angry, scared, and doped African America. Although most African Americans have faced various forms of crisis over the past two decades, no semblance of crisis is portrayed in the book or in its exhibitions, because the organizers chose to emphasize "the hope side of it" (Easter et al. 1992).

To be sure, African America's situation is ripe for hope. Over the last few decades, efforts to enhance mainstream safety have driven many cultural struggles, including that of African Americans, into irrelevancy or obscurity. Two aims of the dominant group have been to delegitimate the social protests of the 1960s and 1970s (e.g., Schor 1986) and to distract attention from the antiracist and decolonizing content of rap music which emerged in the 1970s, 1980s, and 1990s (Baker 1993). To win such struggles, many elites and their institutionally situated professional functionaries sought to control public opinion to such an extent that profound commonalities linking the imagery of events like Hiroshima and the Gulf War in our national consciousness have been comfortably disarticulated in America's mass mind (Pease 1993). Given these persistent attempts to govern what mass audiences think, we cannot presume that the corporate and federal sponsors of *Songs of My People* knowingly invested in an exhibition proposal if its visual content too effectively countered dominant white, male, national values and assumptions.

In fact, the editor/organizers countered "negative" dominant group assumptions while reinforcing the idea that African America largely behaves positively, like most Americans. To accomplish this goal, the editors/organizers selected a rather homogeneous set of images, which, in constellation, tend to reify and ratify an acceptable mainstream portrayal of African-American life. This does little or no justice to diverse African-American experiences. They selected images that suggest to these authors that striving African Americans are doing well in the United States, despite the few social problems faced by a few black people who are not striving hard enough to pull themselves up by their own bootstraps. We see such meanings being constructed through a number of discursive moves. They are embedded in the editor/organizers' image selections, which encourage and legitimate those African Americans who subscribe to mainstream forms of American discipline and deny legitimacy to those who prefer to engage in "the forms of anti-discipline and resistance conducted in everyday life" (Gilroy 1993:103).

We could say that African America's capacity to perfect mainstream forms of discipline are highlighted. For example, some images valorize consumer-oriented socialization practices that have tended to "mainstream" many African Americans.[15] Vicariously, through our children, we celebrate our own youthful socialization experiences in imagery of American conspicuous consumption rituals like our children's high school prom (156–157), our children's school graduations (135, 164), or our own high school reunions (6). But these are not images in which we simply celebrate our youth or our hard-won right to education. They are also moments when we reminisce on hopeful moments of our own youth when we could not yet recognize the glass ceiling, so unfulfilled dreams seemed possible.

Many images legitimate mainstream America's nuclear family model. "Black family" images range across class, from several professional families, who seem to be doing quite well (162–163) to a singular homeless family (170–175). Mainstream family values are affirmed. A few image-instances depict African-American destitution but with fewer clues about its impact on family cohesion. A glimpse into black poverty is also pictured with black intimacy and complacency, or with black-on-black violence. Poverty issues are not visually associated with the competitive practices or Western organization by which American "success" is made accessible only to a growing and small, but increasingly significant, segment of the African-American population (Page 1995). Furthermore, the prideful image of upwardly mobile and stable black family life, though appealing, is less than precise, even among professional black families. Recent book-length essays and novels by mainstream African Americans expose their vulnerability as black professionals (e.g. Cary 1991; McCall 1994; Nelson 1993), explore their rage as members of the black middle class (Cose 1993), examine their disappointment with the failures of the civil rights movement (Bell 1987, 1992), and insist on the necessity of confronting authority in a racial state (Bell 1994). However, not one image in *Songs of My People* speaks to this highly complex and volatile experiential reality.

We see a black woman, giving birth to a healthy child, who is depicted with her husband (181–183), but viewers must skip from the young black newlyweds to a mature interracial couple, and then to this couple giving birth without also linking the sequence to images of pregnant African-American women. The one pregnant woman we do see elsewhere in the book is situated in rural poverty and is not celebrated as someone who is viably reproducing "the race" (128–129). Anyone following this hopeful jazz conversation may be shocked, immediately following the healthy birth, to see another lone black woman giving birth to a 3–pound "crack baby" who requires emergency medical treatment (184–185). Oddly, the emphasis rests not on the mother and her child, but on the hospital services now provided to blacks, often through the professionalism of black doctors. In another image, a black mother's child is treated by a black physician in a rural clinic, highlighting his commitment to serving needy black clients. Yet, no image reveals the African-American mothers who vigilantly try to guard their children's health from the frequent iatrogenic effects of medical treatment.

The editor/organizers ignore a variety of long-term unions that are also being celebrated in African-American communities with increasing frequency and without legal marriage, including heterosexual, bisexual, lesbian, gay, and transsexual couples. Alternate styles of extended households, unrelated households, female-headed households, or differently gendered households organization are not included. The unacceptability of these black options is suppressed. The message is that such images, no matter how frequently they occur in our actual population, would not amount to an acceptable mainstream portrayal of African American life. In contrast, we witness a beautiful and intimate Western-style marriage ritual, portrayed in an elegant wedding shot by Roy Lewis (178). But the picture is strangely entitled "jumping the broom," as if the dress styles and manner of ritual practice depicted directly refer to a syncretized African wedding tradition rather than a basically European one. A dominant discourse is reproduced when this state-sanctioned style of marriage is allowed to stand as the only way that African Americans marry or cohabitate. Other styles of black marriage or cohabitation are excluded, especially the proliferation of African influenced weddings that have taken place over the past fifteen years and have been popularized in the mass media with black audiences like *Essence* or *Ebony* magazines.

Instead of contrasting black newlyweds with the enduring contentments and difficulties experienced by a more stable mature black couple, an image by Roland L. Freeman jars us into confronting an interracial couple (179). The caption explains that they live in the French Quarter and run an art gallery. More than exploring our participation in interracial coupling, this image depicts an acceptable parameter of our diversity, but it invites no reflection on what quality of love or what forms of black-on-black gender oppression or racialized political economic circumstances might have motivated that particular southern black woman's decision to marry a white man. Depicting a range of blacks who establish different unions across other ethnic/racial lines would help African America grapple more compassionately with all interracial couples, especially where those couples assume an anti-racist stance and intimately embrace African-American community life. However no imagery suggests that the number of interracial marriages is increasing and may be indicative of a trend.[16]

Another category of images refers to violence, either the out-of-control illegal kind or the state sanctioned variety. African Americans in the military assert our participation in and loyalty to U.S. society by countering the commonly held mainstream perception that blacks are less patriotic than whites. When examining military images, we found that all efforts to depict black patriotism are strained. African America's patriotic commitment to military discipline is uncritically celebrated in *Songs of My People* just as it was in the film *Glory*, which was coincidentally released just a few weeks before the Gulf War began on Martin Luther King's birthday. In the selected imagery, young black men are being toughened by white commanding officers during military training (56) and are being trained to exterminate or subdue state-defined "enemies." In addition, we must read such images with the additional understanding that disciplined military training and the honor that should come with military service, should help a black man become a more entitled American man (54–55).

But the entitlement of black men is up for grabs in real life. Some black military men, like the celebrated Colin Powell (120), are entitled to dance with the first lady. Most black military men would never be equally entitled. As President George Bush once declared, "Gulf War veterans were safer in the Middle East than in the streets of their own cities" (Pease 1993:564). This is an admission that blacks who live on most city streets are less entitled. Economic and public policies implemented by the black soldiers' hidden "enemies" in the United States tend to devastate black communities over decades (see Bluestone and Harrison 1982:3–12). When those soldiers come home to unemployment, drugs, and homelessness, armed with military skills and a will-to-kill, in moments of extreme frustration, they may be apt to turn their military expertise on their own communities.[17]

While patriotic African Americans like Colin Powell have always sought entitlement by contributing honorable military service to our nation, young black males frequently used the military option not necessarily because they are patriotic, but as a desperate last resort before encountering the kind of trouble on neighborhood streets that could lead to jail or death. Remarkably, conditions have not changed since the Civil War when joining the military was the only sure way to get food and clothes. The violent context of urban black residential life could be depicted with reference to black military participation and explained not in terms of young black men's shameful personal failure or simply their growing lack of economic opportunity, but increasingly, in terms of their regular experience of random police harassment, whether or not they are involved in illicit activities.

In fearful and frustrated moments, the police may accidentally kill or unjustly lock up young black males, in the name of keeping the peace.[18] At the same time, a growing number of black community meetings against police violence are not depicted. Nor are those African-American families who battle routine hostile judicial practices depicted. Such motivations for joining the military are visually neglected and patriotism is not a prerequisite. Yet, *Songs of My People* gives no indication that such conditions may recruit many African-American youth into the military. For many, it becomes a situation of escape in which one can acquire room, board, and meals, and a legal income unavailable for the unemployed in their home community. In the absence of domestic tranquillity, many urban African Americans live in residential war zones and share a daily fear (49) of their own young men who engage in illicit activities that they hope will help them "make it" in America. Too many of those young men, who are likely to succeed at illicit activity, grow idle and become steeped in the inaction of despair (46). That is why we assign military images (54–57) to our violence-related category which includes other violence-generative images such as gang members (48–49), drug-related death (pp. 168–169), police action (p. 47), and incarceration (50–53), widely believed to curtail violence.

By showing African Americans "hard at work," like real Americans are supposed to be, the organizers counteract the media perception that blacks are less hardworking than European or Asian Americans. This is seen in photographs of blacks "hard at work" in images of three elderly people: a teacher (201), a writer (124), and a farmer (194). But one image of the black hardwork ethic is reproduced among black youth (197). No black youth who manage to find and keep jobs that supplement household incomes are shown at work for minimum wage at McDonald's, at a car wash, or at a local bank. Occupational images show some working people hard at work, but ordinary African Americans are not seen prospering at well-paid jobs. We do see, or at least, we presume, the prosperity and social stature of well-paid professionals like athletes (94,95,97), artists (68,69,131), models (146), politicians, construction workers (38–39) and possibly the endangered black farmers who often own their land (188–197). On the least prosperous side, we see a small-town coal miner (28), low-wage farm workers (190), circus artists (80–81), showgirls (82), and subway and street car musicians (ii, 5, 76). Except for policemen and incidental nurses, we do not see a whole level of occupational practice among people who work at mundane jobs such as tellers, clerks, secretaries, child-care workers, drug abuse counselors, or postal delivery people. African Americans struggled for admission into craft and trade unions and fought as union members in labor movements over decades across the nation, yet there are no images that pay homage to the worker-resistance aspect of our lives. Skilled blue-collar workers are portrayed less often than unskilled laborers, unemployed people and white collar professionals. In addition, more white-collar workers are depicted than any other workers, allowing foreigners who view this exhibition to presume that most African Americans must do that kind of work.

Many work images reveal African America's confusion about the role of schooling in preparing us for American success. One image of a student studying (134) describes her "cramming" for a test, not seeking to really learn and understand. No images show black students in conference with professors at historically black institutions or at predominantly white institutions. None portrays deeply engaged black students working in study groups or questioning lecturers who come to speak at their schools. None features black university students tutoring younger African-American high school or grade school students with a fierce determination to be competent. We see "cramming," we see a bit of in-class work (200, 202), and we see students graduating (x, 204, 205), but we do not see students involved in any self-initiated learning activity like going to the neighborhood library. Finally, where are the black students who fail? Where are the otherwise brilliant ones who get no educational credentials because they end up studying in jail, like Malcolm X, and what about those who are relegated to learning-disabled classes? Where are those who would rather shoot craps for lunch money than go to class where, from their perspective, you learn irrelevant material? Where are the students who write parodic raps about a few tedious and often racist teachers whom they dislike? In other words, the often tenuous link between hard work in school and occupational outcomes could have been explored more deeply.

A greater focus on men than on women may reflect the perceptual inclinations of the editor/organizers, or it may reflect the intent of a few male and female photographers who decided to highlight black men.[19] In either case, image-instances of men occur 1.5 times more often than those of women. While men are sole subjects in 28% of the gendered images, women are shown alone half as often, in only 14% of the images (Table 5.2). Images of men with other men represent 48% of the image-instances while 21% show women together. Although this pattern may be unintentional, the strong presence of men either at work, with family, with friends, or just having fun stands in sharp contrast to the several men depicted on the street, in prison, or in the military. We do not question the sex ratio in numerous image-instances and its social implications. For example, the visual gender pattern representing children mirrors the adult pattern (Table 5.3). A fourth of the image-instances show male and female children together, and another fourth show female children only. In contrast, sole male children are shown half the time, male-children are shown with female children a fourth of the time, and female children are shown without male children only a fourth of the time.

We found a similar pattern in which a third of the children are accompanied by men, another third by women and men, but less than a third of the children by only women. At a rate of 64%, female children were unaccompanied by any adult, while male children were accompanied by adults at the same rate. So, why are female children less often shown and less often accompanied by adults? Why are men more often shown with children than women?

Class-based representations of gender in the professional workplace extend this gender bias (Table 5.4). Although the total number of professional images is small (N=12), images of white collar occupations depict professional males three times more often than professional women. Four out of six female professionals are depicted with male professionals and, among all the professionals, only two (16%) of the images show women alone whereas six (50%) of the images portray men alone. The subtle message is twofold: (1) female African-American professionals "don't make it on their own" without a male prop, and (2) the mythical dominative power of African-American women is best subdued by men.   A similar visual pattern emerges in the gender balance among artists (including performers and musicians) and artisans (Table 5.5). Artistic males are depicted four to five times more often than females.

Table 5.2
Images-Instances of African Americans by Gender (N=197)

Image-Instance	Number	%	% of Difference	M/F Proportional Difference
Males present	156	79		
Females present	101	51	28	1.5
Sole male	56	28		
Sole female	28	14	14	2.0
Males only	96	48		
Females only	41	21	27	2.3

Table 5.3
Image-Instances of African-American Children by Gender and Adult Companions (N=50)

					Gender of Adult Companionship			
No. Child. by Gender	No.	%	% Child. Unaccompanied	% Child. Accompanied	Male	Female	Both	Sum
Sole male	27	54	37	63	6	5	6	17
Sole female	11	22	64	36	1	1	2	4
Both	12	24	25	75	2	3	4	9
Totals	50	100	40	60	9	9	12	30

We do not suspect the editor/organizers of intentionally subordinating female imagery in favor of male imagery. Nor do we presume that the photographers provided such a narrow range of gendered imagery. We do believe that this gender bias may or may not have been present in the original set of images. If it was not, then it could very well be an effect of the image-selection process which intended to affirm the place of black men in America's prevailing gender ideology by disaffirming racial ideologies that typically portray the same men in such a negative light. In a telephone interview, one editor/organizer reported that female photographers encouraged the emphasis on male imagery, but a female photographer to whom we spoke refused to confirm his claim.

Table 5.4
African-American Professionals by Gender (N=12)

Image-Instance	No.	%
Sole male	6	50
Sole female	2	16
Male and female	4	33

Table 5.5
African-American Artists by Gender (N=32)

Gender	Number	%
Male	24	75
Female	5	16
Male and female	3	9

THE EMBEDDED STORY

The organizers warned us not to expect symphonic coherency among all the pictures and insisted that "No one picture tells the whole story" (Easter et al. 1992:ix). However, the coherent and embedded story they do tell is forewarned in the introduction by noted photojournalist and visual activist, Gordon Parks. He advised us to look only for art (Easter et al. 1992:xi). By implication, we should not look for a social justice message or for any critique of American social policy. In the spirit of collegiality, Parks concedes authority to the editor/organizers' uncritical approach and defends each photographer's artistic freedom by explaining that "The heart, not the eye seems to have determined the contents of their photographs. What their eyes saw was one thing; what their heart perceived was yet another" (Parks, in Easter 1992:xiii). However poetically, he warns that the images are not in parallax; that is images cast onto eyes observing African America in real life were not reconciled with images cast onto hearts that photographically expressed themselves. Parks explains this lack of a parallax image by suggesting that "All of the contributors were born to a childhood of confusion" (xiii). Racial confusion is one outcome of the information they actively consumed through church, school, work, or even in the military. These institutional sites of cultural struggle shaped the formation of their personal identities in social terms that may have predisposed them to narrowly construe and portray a national range of African-American identities.

Parks's discomfort with the embedded story is revealing. On the one hand, he admits that the contributors "transcended the limitations that might have been wrongly ascribed to their birthright" (xiii). On the other hand, in the same

Dizzy Gillespie-like breath, he fears that "We need miracles now" (xiii). Furthermore, he warns that these images do not constitute the miracle he had in mind. In a graceful signifying gesture, he indirectly suggests that the selected images fail to depict the crises that his own eyes cannot escape. He sees proof of this failure in the first image, by Keith Hadley, on the cover of the First Edition (also see 177). People might see that picture and say "what a pretty little girl," but this schoolgirl, with her African braids punctuated by European berets, is looking from behind an American flag. Parks seems to believe, as we do, that this little girl, at the tender age of 9, already knows what the American flag holds in store for her. Does she not already have knowledge of unequal chances, despite the organizers' caption (Easter et al. 1992:177) which claims that she wants to become a doctor? When Parks described this image (Easter et al. 1992:xi), he wrote, "The sad eyes of a little girl, lifted toward the lens for a second, reflect the stars on our country's flag, while seeming to also reflect the darkness of the morning wrapped around her."

Furthermore, Parks admonishes that "we [African Americans] must nourish a need to excel through our African heritage" (Easter et al. 1992:xiii)[20] but in *Songs of My People* African identity is subdued by American education and occupational success. Black dancers of European ballet are shown, but not black dancers in the African, Latin, or Caribbean tradition. Why show black New Orleans jazz musicians or black conductors of Western classical orchestral music without showing black African drummers? Why are there no African musicians of popular contemporary music except Quincy Jones (69) and Urban Bush Women (9)? Why show black people engaged in Western forms of business without showing black tradesmen and tradeswomen hawking their wares at African cultural festivals or at family reunions, or why not show some of the rejuvenating cultural and development activities sponsored by black community organizations or by African-American libraries or bookstores?

Although some images express African elements of spirituality, the Africa-colonizing Judeo-Christian-Islamic traditions predominate throughout the images (18, 23, 104–113, 115, 199). The Islamic influence is acknowledged, but its rapidly growing influence is still downplayed. African-oriented Diaspora religious practices are mostly ignored. The organizers promote themselves as cultural experts, but offer no images of Santeria rituals or practitioners so easily located in major coastal cities like New York, Miami, and Los Angeles. The only exception is one image, by C. W. Griffin, showing a voodoo priest (114), but his role in the community is not made clear. Is he just an eccentric old man, or is he really a voodoo priest? If so, then why is he not depicted with his congregation or clients? Why is he depicted, out of context, merely as an individual (on the uses of dominant visual representation of individualism, see Bambara 1994:136), ungrossed in the ritual activity of ministering to people whose lives he serves?

African-American body aesthetics are similarly cross-dislocated. Compare the photographs captioned "Shades of Beauty," by Kirk McKoy (145) and "The Three Physicians," by D. Michael Cheers (149). In this attempt to depict the spectral range of African beauty, two culturally recognizable and differently valued phenotypical features are represented. In "Shades of Beauty," African-American viewers are encouraged to accept images of three women as if they exemplify our aesthetic taste in physical beauty. While the organizers might prefer the physical features of those women that is, "the keen, noble slope of their delicate noses," and their medium to thin lips, accentuated with an emphasis on relatively light, peolan skin tone, others may like the beautiful women physicians depicted on page 149. In a national context where we learn as children that a white appearance is a right appearance, the embrace of dark color and kinky hair has not come easy. Finally, why does the beauty of male bodies go unnoted?

EXHIBITIONARY DISCIPLINE AND CONTAINED AFRICAN-AMERICAN IDENTITY

Stuart Hall identifies African-American efforts to construct "successful" counter-identities through popular culture as a problem that can undercut African America's effectiveness in the cultural struggle. We may find ourselves constructing counter-identities, like the "black man identity," for example, that can cross-dislocate the black sense of manhood in ways that are likely to enhance domination, not dismantle it.

Thus, to put it crudely, certain ways in which black men continue to live out their counteridentities as black masculinities and replay those fantasies of black masculinities in the theaters of popular culture are, when viewed from along other axes of difference, [enacted as] the very [dominant white] masculine identities that are oppressive to women, that claim visibility for their [dominant white-male-like] hardness only at the expense of the vulnerability of black women and the feminization of gay black men. The way in which a [dominant] transgressive politics in one domain is constantly sutured and stabilized by reactionary or unexamined politics in another [subordinate domain] is only to be explained by this continuous cross-dislocation of one identity by another, one structure by another. (Hall 1992:31)

As edited here, Hall's insight helps the present writers to suggest that popular black male counter-identities are constructed as cross-dislocations in symbolic opposition to white male identities (also emulated). Subaltern counter-identities are historically constructed in relation to the bearers of elite and elite-functionary dominant identities whose tactics often pit those bearers of subordinate counter-identity against each other. Thus, our groups' quest for inclusionary mainstream sanction often passes judgment on those whose behavior is not appropriately mainstream or those who may not want to be whitened enough even to be regarded as an acceptable bearer of mainstream identity.

Ultimately, the passing of such judgments against each other undermines our collective capacity to grasp and appreciate the full and diverse range of black racial counter-identity politics. As illustration, popular images exalting the black family are usually cross-dislocative representations that sanctify the nuclear family household and obscure the large number of female-headed households in our population. Images giving men center stage cross-dislocate the prominence of women's activity. But the larger insight is not limited to interrogating the counteridentity of African-American men or African-American households. It suggests, more importantly, that all African-American counter-identities are cross-dislocated when constructed in symbolic opposition to European-American identities in ways that inhibit African America's cooperation with other "minority" groups, like Korean America, for instance (Kim 1993).

This point begins to explain why we are witnessing African America's claim to a theoretical set of American rights that so many Americans believe should be denied to other immigrants.[21] African-American elites and the middle-class are starting to support police control of black communities and even advocate capital punishment as a solution to urban black crime. This is not just because of fear, but also because such tactics allow them to avoid direct engagement with subaltern African Americans who failed, or so it seems. In the not too distant past, such tactics were considered fundamentally invasive and indicative of a level of state surveillance and control formerly thought to be supported only by mainstream European Americans. In short, mainstream African Americans most often fail to see how the black counter-identities that we construct as apparent acts of resistance are actually cross-dislocated by a dominant "white" one. This is in the same way that Hall believes African-American male counter-identities are cross-dislocated by questionable alignment with European-American male identities.

To counter the "five deadly ways" that African Americans are portrayed in the mainstream media, the editor/organizers trained their audience to visually conceive of African Americans in five hopeful ways that limit options for interpreting the black experience. Whereas the media depict blacks as "less intelligent," the organizers focused on school, on professionals, on our love for education, and on our respect for skilled ability. Whereas the media suggest that we are less hardworking than European Americans, the organizers emphasized the black presence in the workplace, regardless of class location. While the media suggest that blacks, especially black men, are more prone to violence, the editor/organizers admitted gang behavior, cited police encounters, noted high rates of imprisonment, and disproportionately depicted gentle black men in peaceful family settings, even when the family was homeless.

Of great significance here is the realization that cross-dislocations allow mass audiences to be manipulated through the flow of information from educative/entertaining channels, including the exhibitionary practices of museums and the public relations practices of corporations or federal agencies like the United States Information Services. Increasingly, African America is becoming more familiar with the image-making power wielded by federal or corporate elites (and their media agents). At the same time, it is hard to firmly grasp how elites benefit from black obsession with "positive" black imagery. As active media consumers, African Americans have learned to reject black imagery as "negative" if it publicly makes them feel ashamed in the eyes of mainstream America. Imagery that makes blacks feel proud is regarded as positive. Blacks attribute a judgment of negative black imagery to the subaltern sources of gangsta rap, for example, and they deem mainstream cultural products like *Songs of My People* as positive black imagery.

In negative rap imagery, African Americans—who aspire to achieve or sustain mainstream status—believe that black youth are not portraying African America in a positive way. Blacks question why elite America seeks to profit from such portrayals.[22] In fact, we fear that African America's embarrassing subaltern embrace of rap music will only encourage mainstream America to keep marketing negative black imagery in an effort to enhance any denigrating popular assumptions about black national potential. In contrast, the positive images in *Songs of My People* evoke a sense of pride in black endurance and accomplishment. It predisposes us to believe that enlightened elites and their established organizations promoted *Songs of My People* because they care more about supporting the black collective assertion of equality than agents of dominant society who profit by promoting gangsta rap.

When mainstream African Americans direct their children to *Songs of My People* and away from gangsta rap they may think they are choosing something more edifying, but they are only jumping out of the maligned influence of ghetto fire and into the safety of a high-class frying pan. In either case, their children's minds are exposed to commodified black representations, except those children are never told that rappers may retain a bit more representational autonomy than the photographers who submitted 55,000 images to the *Songs of My People* project. Unlike the frequently embarrassing imagery in gangsta rap, the images in *Songs of My People* look respectable. This may be why few people ever notice that both representational modes similarly undermine the more autonomous acts of cultural production than our audiovisual activists attempt. Few people notice that the same elite, corporate or federal sponsor that chooses to invest in negative gangsta rap is just as likely to invest in positive photographic exhibits like *Songs of My People*. Divergent investment strategies do not necessarily reflect an overtly racist intent, but the dollars linked to contracts and black talent control support the infrastructure of white public space.

A young African-American artist like Tracy Chapman may hit the charts with the fiery lyrics and music of a first album, but is subjected to whitening control when advised to "tone down" or "cross over" (on this topic, see Bambara 1994:132) if she wants to stay in the business and maintain her mainstream audience. Similarly, divergent investments improve the bottom line because they establish and maintain good public relations with various segments of African America's diverse markets. But when the authority to select imagery for preservation and promotion shifts from all-white hands into black hands, then what might it all mean, really? Theoretically, it means blacks must always remember that black visual entrepreneurs are safer than black visual activists in this postindustrial era which is also postcolonial. Thus, the deployment of

Songs of My People must be read as a postcolonial discourse reproducing colonial discursive strategies, now defunct.

When faced with a popular demand for a more "positive" public and better publicized counter-identity for African America, the three associates of New African Visions Incorporated said, "It'll be us!" African-American audiences responded with popular acclamation. But we need to notice that "positive" black imagery can serve the same disciplinary function as negative black imagery. To think about this disciplinary function, we need only to recall colonial images of the savage and exotic black "other." These images were imported to the West and destined for audiences who consumed such imagery in private and commercial white museums. They opened up doors to educate, entertain, and manufacture consent. Then, the terms of the black others exclusion was the subtext of such exhibits, today, these terms comprise the subtext. Select "positive" images of domesticated black others are exported from western locations—as documentary proof of racial progress in the west—and are used to entertain, educate and manufacture consent among members of national and global audiences.

In either of its exhibitionary forms, *Songs of My People* disciplines the mass audience into accepting inclusion on the basis of certain terms by promoting palliative or embraceable images of African Americans who seem most concerned, either about individual achievement or about their household's pursuit of mainstream success. The images also portray hopeful African Americans who may never achieve mainstream status, but who nevertheless accept a life full of success denied. As one young black man who lives in an urban war zone hopelessly told his photographer, "I would love to be living when the book comes out" (48).

But how will his life be if he lives and continues to measure his worth in terms of mainstream success? On the back of the frontispiece, C. W. Griffin depicts a ten-year-old boy blowing the blues on the corner of Toulouse and Royal late in the New Orleans night. If the little girl discussed earlier was anticipating a sad American future, even if she manages to succeed in medicine, then this young boy is already living her sadness as his own very knowledgeable experience of oppression, musically expressed. Yet, the sad young boy's image is contextually assigned a hopefulness that is not assigned to the young adult who anticipates his death. We are to read the boy's image as hoping for the decontextualized "success" of the neurosurgeon (60–63), the music industry giant (69), the professional sports figures (94, 95, 97), the fashion models (17, 146), the professional politicians (121, 122, 123, 166), the orchestral conductor (68), or the legal professionals (116, 119). Through such images, African America's attainment of "success" is equated with dancing with Barbara Bush (120); vacationing at a sea-side resort (153); washing a black-owned Mercedes outside their home in suburbia (167), meriting a sidewalk star in Hollywood (83), or being a Republican cabinet member (33). Ironically, success is never depicted as black professionals getting their hands dirty as they voluntarily try to meet the needs of distressed black communities or work after hours without pay at revitalizing black cultural life. Instead, success is depicted as moving up and out of the black community, unless one stays behind to earn a living by providing costly services. Viewers accept success images that only speak of status acquisition as the same success images which represent the still impermeable barriers which blocked the access of each successful black person and which is still blocking access for most African Americans.

Putatively hopeful images of success in *Songs of My People* also say a lot about the absence of success in black communities, and speaks to the very real cost of trying to attain it. Everyone knows that most African Americans are not targeted for success. Yet, an absence of "success" often leaves blacks confused about the legitimacy of their aspirations, or it leaves them bereft of any aspirations at all. Furthermore, so many of the costs of pursuing success are hidden ones. The graduating schoolgirl pays whenever her mainstream educational values conflict with the African home values of her mother (x). The black barber shop, once a fertile site of adult male debate and generative ideas, pays when its discourse is rendered impotent by neighborhood disintegration (12). After twenty years, "Grocer" Sam is paying, with nothing to show for his labor (14), while Sammy Davis, Jr., paid, for a life lived under extreme racial inequality, with a sidewalk star in exchange for his penniless fame. A "Lite" tap dancer pays by aspiring to Sammy's "success" (77).

We see the cost of absent "success" in old work-abused hands (1). In the man playing a subway harmonica for a living (4–5), in the mickey-moused youth whose head and heart are focused not on solving African America's problems but on the consumer fantasy implicit in Disney imagery (7). Our urban youth pay a cost when they play on the architecturally sculptured waters of corporate grounds because they have no playgrounds of similar coolness or beauty in their own neighborhoods (16). A cost is paid when a whole community cannot afford to keep the historic Howard Theater from running down (19). Although they made life-long contributions to American society, our elders pay a cost with their enduring poverty (20–21). Black males pay when they are phased out of status competition with European American males through crime, killing or jail (46–53) or when they desperately turn to the military as a final phase-out option (54–57). We can see costs exacted when an elderly female jazz singer ends a career, doing the rest of her life in prison (137). And we just have to ask: which young men playing midnight basketball (96) will end up like the regal old man (13) watching his neighborhood decay in front of his rapidly aging eyes—if the gun does not claim them first?

We have argued that the visual entrepreneurs who organized this project understood the racial dynamics of success in postcolonial America because as members of an oppressed group they had the knowledge of cumulative organizational experience (mainly as matriculators of church, schooling and various occupations). Thus, they carefully selected 214 images that would succeed from a total of 55,000, and they presented those images to mass audiences as a self-portrait of African America. We do not claim to have examined behavior *within* organizations. Instead, we treated visual imagery as an artifact of the relations of production which network the editor/organizers, the corporation, the museums, the USIA, and their audiences. We suggest that those established organizations occupy a position that empowers them to diminish, if not undermine, the fledgling organizational success of New African Visions Incorporated by imposing an exclusionary sanction if those black editor/organizers had chosen to behave as black visual activists and had proposed to display effective oppositional imagery that might threaten white public space. Instead, the visual entrepreneurs preferred to display hopeful progress.

Finally, we also examined both the categories used to organize the images and the language used when the editor/organizers were insisting that they had no story to tell. We have demonstrated that they are obviously telling a story of mainstream success for African Americans in an effort to counter "negative" mainstream media representations that have so often portrayed African Americans as incapable of success. We end by characterizing *Songs of My People* as a postcolonial instrument of the exhibitionary complex. It was established to entrain the consent of lower class British audiences to the extravagances of the British Empire by rewarding with civilized (racial) status their counter-identities as good workers and as good consumers of imperial goods. The African-American counter-identity created by this imagery and marketed through museum venues is trying to prove that African America is mainstream material and is not a population of misfits and deviants. The editor/organizers succeeded, but they also blindly end up reproducing the same relations of domination (which allow only some blacks to succeed while disallowing the possibility of domestic tranquillity for most blacks). In other words, we believe that the editor/organizers not only sought to personally succeed, but also needed their mainstream audience to see African America succeeding too. To be safe, they inadvertently trimmed unwanted diversity out of their self-portrait. A bit of African America's experiential ugliness is left in for the sake of attempting to be honest, but overall, the selected imagery represents a set of highly sanitized mainstream categories to be consumed by a postcolonial mainstream audience. We argue that this organizationally successful and sanitized selected imagery makes the project attractive for export to overseas audiences by a federal agency of information control.

NOTES

1. *Songs of My People*, a project of New African Visions Incorporated, organized by the Corcoran Gallery of Art in Washington, D.C., circulated by the Smithsonian Institution Traveling Exhibition Service, and on national tour from September 1992 through November 1994.

2. It is important for readers to know the scope of this exhibit's national exposure. In 1992 it toured Washington, D.C., Los Angeles, Philadelphia, Atlanta, Tampa, Columbus, and New York City. It moved to Chicago in January of 1993. It was seen in Denver from March through May, in Detroit from June to August, in Little Rock from April to May, in Cincinnati in June through August, in Jackson, Mississippi from

August to October, in Memphis from October through December, and in Milwaukee from September to November. New Orleans viewed the exhibit from December through March of 1994. The rest of the 1994 itinerary included Kansas City, Missouri from March to May, Rochester, New York from July to August, San Diego from March to May, Raleigh, North Carolina from June to July, Houston from the end of August through the end of November and St. Louis, Missouri from the end of September to the end of November. For details call the Smithsonian Institution News, 202/357–3178 or Time Warner Community Relations, 212/ 522–1485.

3. I first developed the concept of white public space with reference to my ethnographic research on black access to Tuberculosis–control services in Boston (Page 1994; Page and Thomas 1994). From there, I expanded my understanding of the concept in a paper presented at the Language and Nation conference at UC Davis, entitled From White Identity to the Academic Privileges of White Public Space: Rodney King Themes and Strategic Racial Subordination in the Postcolonial State. In that essay, I argued that white public space represents the means by which those who share ideological whiteness and benefit from white privilege manage to occupy geographic and symbolic territory both in the nation and transnationally. That space may entail particular or generalized locations, sites, patterns, configurations, tactics or devices which routinely, discursively, and sometimes coercively, protect the accrued advantages of whites over nonwhites. Its material resources are often organized through formidable institutions run mainly by professionals who administer the territories they claim or manage the markets they control. In the form of observable material objects, white public space provisions privileged professionals both with implements and infrastructure (e.g., paychecks, offices, computers, examination tools, tele-communications equipment).

4. Although black popular culture is always African and American, the United States has historically sought to control or suppress the Africanness through mainstreamed "negative" and "positive" images of the black body (except in some theater, music or dance). The problem of whiteness and the practices that lead to the whitening of African-American Africanness have been examined in relation to the construction of white women's identity by Ruth Frankenberg (1993). It is also explored in relation to the construction of the nation in American literary production by Toni Morrison, who offers the following observation:

Just as the formation of the nation necessitated coded language and purposeful restriction to deal with racial disingenuousness and moral frailty at its heart, so too did the literature reproduce the necessary codes and restriction. Through significant and underscored omissions, startling contradictions, heavily nuanced conflicts, through the way writers people their work with the signs and bodies of this presence—one can see that a real or fabricated Africanist presence was crucial to their [white citizens of the nation] sense of Americanness. (1992:6)

5. Since the 1980s, access has been opened to entrepreneurial minority visual entrepreneurs like Spike Lee, whose visual imagery safely adheres to mainstream expectations and appeals to mainstream markets (Bambara 1994; Baraka 1993). Like Lee, the editor/organizers of *Songs of My People* safely chose to contest the dominant culture's interpretation of shared situations or events, but did not confront such interpretations head-on in any obvious effort to subvert them. Instead, the absence of confrontation in *Songs of My People* relieves the mainstream audience from the work of having to reconcile "negative" representations of African-American people with the "positive" ones selected and displayed.

6. To get an idea of how size limitations constrained the image-selection process, please note that the initial collection of 55,000 images were submitted by the professional photographers. Those images then reduced to 30,000 images, and later, were reduced again to 10,000 and so on, until the final selection process reduced from 500 possibilities to the 214 images found in the book and to the 152 images from which city-specific variations on the national traveling exhibit were drawn.

7. One anonymous press release reports that the editors' intent in producing *Songs of My People* was to change the way others perceive and so often portray the black community in daily news, on television, and in the movies.

8. Anonymous Press Release.

9. It is unclear as to whether those selections were either made or ratified by New African Visions Incorporated.

10.

Success	42	School	18
Racial Cost	58	Absence of logical other	56
Ambivalent interaction	32	Recreational	63
Occupational	94	Ambiguous Intent	29
Relational	42	Female	41
Male	95	Mixed Gender	60
Religion	15		

Total Image-Instances= 645

11. *The Bay Guardian*, February 3, 1993, pp. 32-33.

12. Using the term *jazz* to metaphorically represent their organizational strategy is clever. After all, jazz is a genre of Westernized Africanized music. On the one hand, the term *jazz* rhetorically authenticates the images as truly representative of who African Americans really are as one population of black Diaspora people. On the other hand, the term sheds no light on the organizer's selection process. Without any knowledge of what images were selected and rejected, we cannot know and should not presume that the organizers' choice of images was intended primarily to represent life in America from the "unique perspective of African Americans" (Easter et al. 1992:ix). Other representational intentions also may have been operative. The editor/organizers' underlying assumption is that jazz permits a degree of freed individual expression that "serious," highly structured European symphonic music disallows. Do not expect a coherent story since we set out to organize a *jazz* conversation and not a symphony, they say. Yet, in making this claim they also suggest that we should not expect narrative coherency because, as they imply, the primacy of improvisation is exalted in *jazz*.

13. Jazz improvisation has often been experienced by mainstream audiences as "controlled chaos," but the chaotic anarchy of individual expression is not its signatory feature. Improvisation does not override or deny the story being told through a coherency grounded in collective expression. Two points are significant here. First, the primary feature of *jazz* and other elements of African America's musical tradition is antiphony (call and response). According to Paul Gilroy (1993:78), "It has come to be seen as a bridge from music into other modes of cultural expression, supplying along with improvisation, montage, and dramaturgy, the hermeneutic keys to the full medley of black artistic practices." (For an excellent discussion of the emergence of anti-essentials in black music since Reconstruction see Gilroy 1993:87–110.) Second, noted jazz musician/film actor Branford Marsalis disputes the idea that jazz invites chaotic expression. "You don't play whatever you feel . . . the only freedom is in structure. There is no freedom in dreaming. People who play anything at all can't play anything else. *The music tells you what to play* [italics added]" (The Boston Phoenix, January 8, 1993, Arts

Section, p.7). When the editor/organizers of *Songs of My People* use the term *jazz*, they do not seem to be using the work in this hybrid African-American sense. Instead, they seem to use the term in its Western, American sense of a less coherent ensemble of individualistic expressions.

14. Under the auspices of the USIA and the management of Harrison/Parrott of London, the smallest number of images are touring Europe, parts of the Caribbean, South America, the Pacific Rim, and thirty-nine African countries over the next ten years.

15. When African Americans lived largely outside of or on the fringes of these socialization practices, as we are seen doing in Julie Dash's film, *Daughters of the Dust*, we were considered by mainstream European America, and have learned from our oppression to consider ourselves, primitive, backward, and uncivilized. Yet, we fought for access to and inclusion in those institutionally based socialization experiences, whether they were situated in church, in school, in the "wish" book (mail-order catalogue), or in the town meeting, and we did so because we were denied equal resource access by means of racial segregation practices intended to precipitate racialized economic stratification. Consequently, once we proceeded to civilize ourselves through religion, education, or science as did Viola and Mr. Sneed in *Daughters of the Dust*, we felt victorious and redeemed as Colored (no longer African) citizens of America.

The problem here is that Viola and Mr. Sneed could not construct the counter-identities of civilized colored Americans without intending to forfeit their Africanness. Nana, the Pezant great-grandmother, begged them not to relinquish this. For Viola, to be civilized, saved and educated meant constructing her identity in opposition to those saltwater Africans whose descendant she is. Nana's daughter-in-law, Hagar, declared herself an educated woman and distanced herself from the contaminating concession of Viola and Mr. Sneed to Nana's request. She did not agree that they should all bow to their African identity as much as they were willing to exalt the counter-identity they sought to construct on the mainland. To affirm her rejection of Africanness and her embrace of modern educated Americanness, Hagar refused to ritually kiss the backwards and primitive African amulet that Nana made from ancestral hair and other objects attached to the Bible. All other members of the Pezant family agreed to do that, partly out of respect for Nana and partly from understanding the lesson she was urgently trying to impart before their departure to the U.S. mainland.

16. "Black-white couples increased from 0.1 percent of married couples in 1970 (965,000 in a total of 44,597,000 U.S. couples) to 0.3 percent in 1980, and 0.4 percent in 1989" (Frankenberg 1993:272n).

17. The 1992 urban insurgency in Los Angeles is said to have erupted with much greater tactical precision in the 1990s than was true in the 1960s (Gooding-Williams 1993).

18. Just hours apart two black boys, age 13 and 16, were killed in separate Brooklyn, New York incidents by city policemen who thought the very realistic-looking toy pistols that both boys were playing with were actually assault weapons. Public housing rooftops are often the site of young boys firing toy guns for target practice. Many real shootings are also reported in those sites, so officers are nervous when they go on duty in such locations. One housing project officer who shot the younger boy was seen "openly crying" when he realized what he had done. The younger boy's father "said he had ordered his child not to play with toy guns because of the possibility of mistake by police officers he had warned his son to put the toy away only 90 minutes before the shooting" (*New York Times*, September 1994, Section A, Column 1, p. 1;

Section B, Column 1–6, p. 3). In response, New York Mayor Rudolph W. Giuliani has a plan underway to merge the public housing police with the New York City Police Department (*New York Times*, September 1994, Section B, Column 1, p. 2). And in response to activist pressure by organizations like Alliance for Survival, distribution companies like Toys R Us have finally agreed to stop the sale of toy guns (CNN News Report, October 15, 1994).

19. In the Cochran Exhibit, on display from February 15 to May 3, 1992, 152 images were shown, but less than 10% (N=13) were shot by women photographers.

20. The emphasis on African identity is not an incidence of essentials. We do not presume the existence of an essential African identity to which all blacks may subscribe. Rather, we see blacks in the United States and elsewhere in the Diaspora constructing locally specific forms of identity that draw on African elements, along with European and other elements. This syncretic or hybrid identity is popularly called African or Afrocentric when it exhibits race cognizance (Frankenberg 1993:15, 140, 158). Contrary to popular misperception, its primary feature is not standing in polar opposition to Eurocentrism, but is the subversion of essentialist biological racism and strives for the "positive" re-significance of things that essentialist racism previously despoiled as hatefully African. This not only includes attempts to claim descendancy from civilizations historically designated as non-African, but it also includes the embrace of phenotypic blackness displayed superficially as characteristically African skin colors, hair textures, nose sizes and pronounced buttocks historically denigrated in this nation.

21. Mainstream African Americans, such as the late African-American progressive, Barbara Jordan, may be joining forces with far-right conservatives like Harold Ezell who served under President Reagan as a regional commissioner of the Immigration and Naturalization Service and who helped to frame Save Our State (SOS), a group spearheading Proposition 187. They want to cut off most public services to undocumented immigrants in California. Both are members of President Clinton's Commission on Immigration Reform, scheduled to report in 1997. While Ezell and SOS members would like to restrict immigration by a huge percentage or at least by cutting benefits, Jordan while head of the Commission on Immigration Reform may have intended to help the administration to buffer right-wing demands for immigration control with less stringent interventions. Though perceived through the media as costing taxpayers, the illegal immigrants in California actually add a surplus of $30 billion annually to that state's economy. Yet, in a bid for reelection the Clinton compromise is proposing to make it easier to deport immigrants who get welfare benefits (Marc Cooper, *Village Voice*, October 4, 1994:28–34).

22. To explore the implications of this point, consider the stance of an African-American commentator who appeared on National Public Radio to denounce media agents and corporate elites who profit from gangsta rap. As she argued:

Why and how the [gangsta rap] outlaw became the new hero, while laughing all the way to the bank, is what really upsets me. The royalties these performers will receive from their recordings will make them rich, but there are others behind them, pulling the strings, who stand to profit even more from the making and distribution of these albums.There's a big audience for this music. But aren't there any adults along the corporate record chain willing to take some responsibility for the negative messages behind these tunes? What I want to know is who is at the cultural steering wheel, and where are they trying to take us? (Dawn Amungen, Commentary on Violent and Misogynist

Gangsta Rap. "All Things Considered." National Public Radio, Tuesday, December 21, 1993)

REFERENCES

Baker, H.A. 1993. *Black Studies, Rap, and the Academy.* Chicago: University of Chicago.
Baraka, A. 1993. Spike Lee at the Movies. In Mantia Diawara, ed., *Black American Cinema.* New York: Routledge, pp. 145–153.
Bambara, T.C. 1994. Reading the Signs, Empowering the Eye: Daughters of the Dust and the Black Independent Cinema Movement. In Mantia Diawara, ed., *Black American Cinema.* New York: Routledge, pp. 118–144.
Barth, F. 1989. The Analysis of Culture in Complex Societies. *Ethnos* 3–4:120–142.
Behar, R. 1993. Expanding Boundaries of Anthropology: The Cultural Criticism of Gloria Anzaldua and Marlon Riggs. *Visual Anthropology Review* 9(2):83–91.
Bell, D.A. 1987. *And We Are Not Saved: The Elusive Quest for Racial Justice.* New York: Basic Books.
———. 1992. *Faces at the Bottom of the Well: The Permanence of Racism.* New York: Basic Books.
———. 1994. *Confronting Authority: Reflections of an Ardent Protester.* Boston: Beacon Press.
Blueston, B. and Harrison B., eds. 1982. *The Deindustrialization of America: Plant Closings, Community Abandonment and the Dismantling of Basic Industry.* New York: Basic Books.
Cary, L. 1991. *Black Ice.* New York: Vintage Books.
Cose, E. 1993. *The Rage of a Privileged Class: Why Are Middle Class Blacks Angry: Why Should America Care.* New York: Harper.
Easter, E., Cheers, D.M. and Dudley M. Brooks. 1992. *Songs of My People. A Catalogue of the Exhibition.* New York: Little Brown and Co.
Frankenberg, R. 1993. *White Women, Race Matters: The Social Construction of Whiteness.* Minneapolis: University of Minnesota Press.
Gilroy, P. 1993. *The Black Atlantic: Modernity and Double Consciousness.* Cambridge, Mass.: Harvard University Press.
Gooding-Williams, R., ed. 1993. *Reading Rodney King/Reading Urban Uprising.* New York: Routledge.
Hall, S. 1992. What Is the "Black" in Black Popular Culture? In G. Dent, ed., *Black Popular Culture.* Seattle, Wash.: Bay Press.
Halleck, D. and Magnan, N. 1993. Access for Others: Alter (Native) Media Practice. *Visual Anthropology Review* 9(1): 154–163.
Kim, E.H. 1993. Home Is Where the Ham Is: A Korean-American Perspective on the Los Angeles Upheavals. In R. Gooding-Williams, ed., *Reading Rodney King/Read-ing Urban Uprising.* New York: Routledge.
Masilela, N. 1993. The Los Angeles School of Black Filmmakers. In M. Diawara, ed., *Black American Cinema.* New York: Routledge.
McCall, N. 1994. *Make Me Wanna Holler: A Young Black Man in America.* New York: Random House.
Moore, S.F. 1987. Explaining the Present: Theoretical Dilemmas in Processual Ethnography. *American Ethnologist* 14(4): 727–736.

Morrison, T. 1989. Unspeakable Thinks Unspoken: The Afro-American Presence in American Literature. *Michigan Quarterly* 28(1): 1–34.

———.1992. *Playing in the Dark: Whiteness and the Literary Imagination.* Cambridge, Mass.: Harvard University Press.

Nelson, J. 1993. *Volunteer Slavery: My Authentic Negro Experience.* Chicago: Noble Press.

Page, H.E. 1994. White Identity and Institutional Privilege in White Public Space: Controlling Politicized Black Bodies Through Healthy Racial Subordination. Presented at the Annual Meeting of the American Ethnological Society.

———. 1995. *African America's Impotent Observer.* Forthcoming.

Page, H.E. and Thomas, R.B. 1994. White Public Space and the Construction of White Privilege in U.S. Health Care: Fresh Concepts and a New Model of Analysis. *Medical Anthropology Quarterly* 8(1): 109–116.

Pease, D.E. 1993. Hiroshima, the Vietnam Veterans War Memorial, and the Gulf War: Post-National Spectacles. In A. Kaplan and D. Pease, eds., *Cultures of United States Imperialism.* Durham, N.C.: Duke University Press.

Schor, I. 1986. *Culture Wars: School and Society in the Conservative Restoration, 1969–1984.* Boston: Routledge and Kegan Paul.

Sider, G. 1994. Identity as History: Ethnohistory, Ethnogenesis and Ethnocide in the Southeastern United States. *Identities* 1(1): 109–122.

Therborn, G. 1985. *The Ideology of Power and the Power of Ideology.* New York: Routledge, Chapman, and Paul.

Wallace, M. 1990. Modernism, Postmodernism and the Problem of the Visual in Afro-American Culture. In *Out There: Marginalization and Contemporary Cultures.* Cambridge, Mass.: MIT Press.

Williams, B. 1995. The Public I/Eye: Conducting Fieldwork to Do Homework on Homelessness and Begging in Two U.S. Cities. *Current Anthropology* 36(1): 25–51.

CHAPTER 6

African-American Cultural Nationalism
Yvonne V. Jones

Within the past decade African Americans in the United States have undergone a cultural revitalization that may be seen as a continuation of the black power/black pride movement that emerged during the 1960s civil rights era. Accompanying the judicial and legislative enactments illuminated by historians such as Branch (1988), Garrow (1988), and Carson (1981) was the popularization of African culture articulated in various arenas of a diverse African-American community: the revitalization movement of black Muslims, a student-driven movement of black power advocates (Hamilton and Carmichael 1967), a black separatist movement advocating violence as a means of achieving racial equality (Brown 1993), and a cultural movement, which in the 1960s emerged out of scholarly discourse (Karenga 1993). These diverse movements, each with its distinct ideologies, was accompanied by the acceptance of African influence on the cultural traditions of African Americans, and an embracing of the theories of Herskovits and the repudiation of Franklin Frazier's cultural conservatism (Cole 1985). This chapter examines African-American cultural nationalism as a cultural phenomenon and as a creative, productive practice in a midsize metropolitan city of the Upper South, Louisville, Kentucky. The chapter is divided into three parts. The first part examines the juxtapositioning of race, space, and place in the discourse constructed by the visual and print media of Louisville and replicated and reinterpreted in the discourse embedded in public policy with respect to the city's black community. The second part focuses on two aspects of African-American social organization, Kwanzaa celebrations and the local chapter of a scholarly voluntary association in which racial/cultural identity has assumed a distinct Diaspora posture (African victim of European exploitation). Finally, the relationship between African-American cultural production and a distinct pattern of entrepreneurship is analyzed.

INTRODUCTION

Black performance and aesthetic communities experienced similar changes. Literature written by black authors and playwrights came to the attention of white publishers to a degree not seen since the Harlem Renaissance. James Baldwin and Leroy Jones, whose works signaled the attention of white audiences via best-seller lists and Broadway productions, are examples. Black artists also underwent a transformation as African artistic styles became more pronounced in their work, and they became vocal advocates of using art and performance as a form of social protest. White patronage spawned the emergence of storefront museums, art exhibits (Fine 1973), and street fairs (Hazzard-Gordon 1990).

These diverse movements achieved a degree of commonality through overlapping networks, performance milieus, and other vehicles of black popular culture as primarily young, urban, college-educated blacks adopted African clothing, naming practices, decorative arts, and African itineraries and experimented with various "African" or "natural" hairstyles. This cultural shift was also shaped by international events, most notably the Vietnam War's impact on urban black communities. This took place when males returned as embittered veterans or in coffins and in African and other Third World independence movements to dismantle European colonialism. These national and international struggles merged with the movement of previous eras, specifically with Pan Africanism, a cultural and political movement linking Africans on the continent and in the Diaspora through common cultural traditions and experiences of slavery, colonialism, and oppression. Finally, the immigration of blacks from the Caribbean and Central America to the metropolitan cities along the Atlantic coast stimulated interest in the African Diaspora and infused the African-American community with their cuisine, music, and social organization (Kasinitz 1992; Laguerre 1984). More important than the outward symbols of ethnic identity which these Africans of the British, French, Dutch and Hispanic colonies of the Caribbean Basin brought with them into the metropolitan cities of the Atlantic coast were their shared position within the capitalistic axis and their common symbols representing opposition to this structuring. This was embodied in distinct personalities such as W.E.B. Du Bois, known internationally in black communities as the father of Pan Africanism, Marcus Garvey, a Jamaican migrant and advocate of black economic autonomy and migration back to the African continent, Claude McKay, the Jamaican-born author of the Harlem Renaissance, and C.L.R. James, Trinidad-born historian, Pan Africanist and socialist thinker.

Manning Marable and Leith Mullings's model of racial ideology allows us to situate this latest postmodern nationalism within the contours of the historical development of black political struggles and philosophies. They identify three overlapping "strategic visions" within African-American culture: (1) an inclusive or pragmatic individualism that seeks a "color–blind" society and full participation in economic, political, and social arenas of American life; (2) a separatist vision, stressing cultural, political and economic autonomy; and (3) a radical democratic vision that seeks to eliminate those institutions that perpetuate power and privilege. Separatist strategies, they contend, become a dominant mode of discourse when economic expansion is uneven; when both parties tilt to the right of the political spectrum; when there is an increase in racist violence; and when the inclusionist black political leadership and middle class embrace the status quo (Marable and Mullings 1994:68–69).

Reminding us that separatist visions advance when inclusive strategies retreat, their conclusions allow us to view the growth of this most recent expansion of cultural nationalism alongside the increasing conservative character of both national parties and the legislative assaults on affirmative action and immigration policies. The distinctive character of African-American cultural nationalism at this juncture is embellished by several factors that give it its postmodern tone. The first is its class-inclusive character, which has drawn from key segments of African Americans: the working class, hip hop, college-educated, professional, intellectual, and performance elites. Their familiarity with Africa at this juncture is in large part due to the continent's accessibility, via air transport, and indirectly through art and artifacts, magazines, the media, and recording milieu. Within this context, Africa's commodification has enhanced its accessibility. In the context of praxis, the intersection of divergent class segments of African Americans is illuminated through the literary genre of Gloria Naylor's *Women of Brewster Place* (1983). Located in a northern city, the site itself owed its existence to the malevolent actions of the city's political and economic elites and by the 1960s it became the object of settlement of southern black refugees. Having thus situated Brewster Street historically in the preface, Naylor presents seven black women, one of whom, Kiswana, embodies the overlapping complexities of Marable and Mullings's (1994) inclusive and separatist racial visions.

The daughter of a black middle-class family, Kiswana drops out of college and moves to Brewster Street where she plans to gain financial independence and join the struggles of her low-income neighbors. While this decision causes a schism within her family that is not repaired by the end of the text, she is eventually able to organize a tenants rights organization. The character of Kiswana not only brings community activism to Brewster Street, but she brings her African heritage as well in the form of her name, dress, and hairstyle, and her African values translate to inspire political activism. Naylor therefore integrates class, cultural and political interests into her theme of individual and societal revitalization. Her text captures perfectly the internal dynamics and conflicts present within the African-American community during the civil rights era.

A second factor that lends African-American nationalism its postmodern tone is the Diaspora character present in this more recent version of cultural nationalism. African Americans in the nation's declining urban centers have been joined by immigrants from the Caribbean (Kasinitz 1992; Laguerre 1984; Portes 1994; Sutton and Chaney 1987), and African Americans residing in small towns have interacted with the temporary migrants drawn to its farm economies. While this interactional pattern has been ongoing (Drake and Clayton 1945; Osofsky 1966), more inclusive immigration policies and the declining economic powers of the West have resulted in a significant population increase of West Indians which have become more visible in political and popular culture arenas of African-American society. Increased immigration from Africa, actions of black missionaries (Mahaniah 1982; Phiri 1982; Williams 1982), and periodic political appeals from African leaders (e.g., Haile Selassie's antifascist appeal to the League of Nations in 1939 and Nelson Mandela's appearance at Yankee Stadium, in 1990) increased African-American view of Africa as their homeland. Federal, municipal and college exchange programs have brought about a more intensive and interactive pattern between the U.S. mainland, island and continental Africans.

Third, African-American cultural nationalism has become enjoined to commodization and entrepreneurship, creating distinct markets in local neighborhoods and in some instances challenging the dominance of white and Asian-owned businesses in black communities. Central to this market has been the incorporation of African or African-inspired decorative arts, hairstyles, and clothing into the material culture of African Americans. Used for display in various private and public contexts, these commodities have become central markers of identity and perform integrative functions in uniting separatist, religious and progressive beliefs and elements and thereby minimize gender conflict within cultural nationalist discourse.

Fourth, cultural nationalism has been positioned in the academy as Afrocentric discourse in many Black Studies departments, which were themselves spawned from the urban and civil rights conflicts of the 1960s (Asante 1980, 1988). This intellectual discourse has challenged Eurocentric public school curricula and has sought to construct alternative theories on the cultural origins of Africans and its influence in European, Asian and New World societies (e.g., see Van Sertima 1976, 1985a, 1985b). Having both activist and intellectual dimensions, Afrocentric discourse links the scholars of the academy to grass-roots activists, to religious institutions, and, through the dissemination of texts, to wide sectors of urban working-class and middle-class African Americans. Afrocentric discourse thus challenges the Western hegemonic discourse on race, both in its traditional contexts of rank and primacy and its postmodern embodiment of eugenics and cultural preparedness. Finally, Afrocentricity gives a distinctive character to African-American cultural nationalism, permitting the construction of an alternative identity that challenges the largely demonic image of blackness reflected in many arenas of American life.

This chapter examines African-American cultural nationalism as a cultural phenomenon and as a creative, productive practice as it is constructed in a midsize metropolitan city of the Upper South, Louisville, Kentucky. Located at the falls of the Ohio River, the city's African-American population has encompassed one-third to one-fourth of the city's population from the ante-bellum era to the present. According to the 1990 Census, slightly more than 70% of African Americans reside in racially identifiable neighborhoods west of the city's central business district, and 30% reside in its suburbs where they are concentrated in racially identifiable areas.

While the intellectual dimensions of cultural nationalism have been challenged by scholars (Gilroy 1993; Lefkowitz 1996; Lefkowitz and Rogers 1995), it has been defined here largely through ethnographic observation and practice of the participants themselves. The black Louisvillians who are the focus of this chapter broadly acknowledge the centrality of ancient Egyptian civilization in the subsequent advancement of humanity as a whole, and link local events to international arenas through the prism of an African Diaspora. In specific local practice, cultural nationalism may involve the construction of a distinctive religious ideology in which Afro-Baptist tenants may be juxtapositioned with Islamic or Afrocentric beliefs and traditions, as well as the deliberate formation of an African personality as evidenced by the outward symbols of dress, name changes, and participation in various social gatherings and rituals.

This chapter is divided into three parts. The first part examines the juxtapositioning of race, space and place in the discourse constructed by the visual and print media of Louisville, Kentucky, replicated and reinterpreted in the discourse embedded in public policy with respect to the city's black community. The second part focuses on two aspects of African-American social organizations—Kwanzaa celebrations and the local chapter of a scholarly voluntary association in which racial/cultural identity has assumed a distinct Diaspora posture. That is, the rituals constructed and the ideologies given prominence cross national and international boundaries to embrace a shared historical experience originating out of a noble Africa, victim of European exploitation. This juxtapositioning of nobility and victim is observed in practice as it contests the dominant images of the metropole: crime, poverty, dependency, and blackness through vocal utterances of space/race. Finally, the relationship between African American cultural production and a distinct pattern of entrepreneurship is analyzed.

RACE, SPACE AND PLACE

Since its founding in the 1700s, Louisville's position along the southern border of the Ohio River has played an important part in both its construction of history and its pursuit of economic advancement. During the ante-bellum era, the Ohio River represented the most northern extension of slavery. Harriet Beecher Stowe's *Uncle Tom's Cabin* (1852) used the imagery of the river to convey the dangers the slaves undertook in their quest to freedom. Most recently, Toni Morrison's (1987) fictional character Sethe, of *Beloved*, loses a child to the river she must cross with her family to obtain freedom. The city itself is situated on a small peninsula bordering the Ohio River, forming its northern and western boundaries. Economically, during the ante-bellum era, the city's location placed it at the center of the slave-based economy of the Ohio

River Valley. Its proximity to the Ohio River put it in the center of commerce ranging from the lower Mississippi Valley to the cities of the Northeast. Hence, the river is an important symbol of both the city's ante-bellum traditions and its notions of progress, representing a duality of uncontested heritages. During the Civil War, the economic character of the river was emphasized as the slave state refused to join the Confederacy and allowed the construction of a large fort south of the city which was used as a staging ground for Union Army troops. This duality of slave state and union state is often repeated in popular discourse. It is used to foster a history of benign slavery or even to minimize the presence of slaves in its history. It is used to explain why the city's only statue of a Confederate Army officer faces north, for example. It also allows for the restoration of ante-bellum homes to occur with scant attention to the pivotal role they played in a plantation-based economy.

Correspondingly, the city's African-American population is imagined through the prism of these historical contradictions. The distancing of blacks from the city's ante-bellum history is also reinforced by the absence of white-led racial violence and riots, in contrast to other areas of the state (e.g., see Wright 1990), lynchings, and the fact that blacks maintained their franchise throughout the Reconstruction and segregation eras. The historian George C. Wright's examination of the city's race relations during the early part of the 20th century cited numerous white Kentucky novelists, historians, politicians, newspaper reporters, city boosters, and travelers who concluded that blacks were treated far better in Louisville than in other cities of the Deep South. Yet this perception existed alongside judicially mandated segregated parks, neighborhoods, schools, and other public establishments, as well as laws that restricted black entrepreneurship (Wright 1985).

Wright (1985) termed this cultural contradiction *polite racism* for it involves a distancing and reinterpreting of the role of blacks in the city's history and the perception of an ethnographic present that has eliminated racism from public discourse. This is not to suggest, however, that racism has been eliminated in Louisville, Kentucky. Rather, African Americans have been consigned to a category of invisibility, emerging as criminals, dependents, victims, and complainers, infrequently appearing on news broadcasts and newspapers to interrupt the public's serenity.

Louisville, Kentucky's landscape has historically been shaped by race. Until the early part of this century, blacks resided, as in many southern cities, in neighborhoods shaped by social class rather than race. Louisville's blacks lived next door to, or in close proximity to German, Jewish, Irish, and Syrian immigrants as well as the city's newly arrived white migrants from rural Kentucky. A state law passed in 1907 mandated housing segregation by demanding that no one could move into a city block in which one was a racial minority. By the 1920s, most blacks were concentrated in neighborhoods surrounding the city's downtown enclave of hotels, restaurants, private clubs, and service industries where the majority of blacks secured their livelihood. In the late 1950s urban renewal effectively "whitened" the downtown, a process that was completed in the 1970s when the expansion of private and public hospital complexes in the downtown area eliminated all but the black residents of public housing. Concurrently, during this era white residents moved in increasing numbers to suburban areas of the city and county.

At present, more than 80% of the county's black population resides in a concentrated area known as "The West End"; hence race equals place, a perception reinforced by geographic factors. The city's downtown is located along its northern border, which has historically been the center of commerce since its ante-bellum era. Housing segregation resulted in the black population moving increasingly west of the downtown area, and the urban renewal program of the 1950s reinforced this racial difference through the construction of a six-lane street or boulevard separating the newly constructed and "whitened" downtown from the black residential area. The construction of a federal highway linking the downtown area with its white working-class suburban neighborhoods reinforced this racial landscape, as well as the invisibility of its black population, by making it possible for whites to bypass African-American neighborhoods altogether in their commute between work and home. In fact, the geographical landscape, which has been constructed through the assistance of federal policies of urban renewal and transportation, is commonly thought by blacks to enable whites to surround and control them if necessary.

Despite the high concentration of blacks in the city's "West End," a few whites continued to reside there. Many whites simply never moved in the 1960s when the area black population increased. Other whites turned their domiciles into single-or multiple-family dwellings which they rented to newly arriving black residents. The white working-class enclave of Portland, a separate municipality located northwest of the city's downtown until it was incorporated into the city in the late 1890s, was "blackened" in the 1960s as blacks moved into the area even though their concentration remained sporadic.

This juxtapositioning of race and place constructs "otherness" in Louisville, Kentucky, and determines how blacks throughout the metropolitan area are represented and ranked within a hierarchy of places (Harvey 1993). This is observed in several contexts. First, the place name West End acts to homogenize differences of class, social organization, and historical experience among African Americans. In reality, the West End consists of seven distinct neighborhoods, and use of the term, which did not become part of public discourse until the 1960s, signaled its symbolic opposition to the East End, the city's predominantly white, middle-class residential area. Second is the way in which public, civic events and festivals, which take place in the city's downtown area, are constructed so as to "whiten" the area, thereby making it attractive to the city's suburban residents. The city's riverboats, for example, travel eastward on the Ohio River during its annual boat race during the Kentucky Derby festival. Similarly, the city's annual Derby Parade route travels westward, stopping just short of where the West End begins. Third, the close proximity of downtown to the city's West End has resulted in the area becoming contested space between the city's commercial interests and its black population. The Chamber of Commerce and Downtown Development Association, representing the metropolitan area's white elite, seek to attract both business and suburban white customers into the downtown area. This is a difficult task since the retail and entertainment businesses have taken flight to the suburbs. The downtown functions primarily as a center for commercial enterprise, tourism, government and judicial activities, and "high" culture—theater, opera, and the symphonic orchestra. Its streets are largely vacant after business hours and on weekends. In seeking to reverse this pattern, the Chamber of Commerce stages a series of "downtown festivals" annually. In addition to the festivals surrounding the Kentucky Derby (lasting two weeks), the city's political and commercial elites sponsor a Charles Dickens fest at Christmas time, a Light-Up Louisville fest at Thanksgiving signaling the arrival of the holiday season, Thunder Over Louisville, a fireworks display, signaling the beginning of Derby festivities, and the German fest during the summer months. These urban festivals create an image conducive to the tourism and convention market that the city wishes to attract; for the great majority of white residents in the metropolitan region, they become their only reason for going downtown.

This urban marketing strategy can be successful only if white residents are persuaded that they will be safe at events located in close proximity to the city's West End. Hence, the threat of crime becomes an underlying, unspoken anxiety, surrounding these events, necessitating proclamations from public officials on the number and positioning of police, the availability of parking spaces, and free public transportation to outlying parking sites. This crowd-managing, crime-managing strategy, of course, is necessary to counter the image of the West End created by the local visual news media.

Television newscasts not only highlight and categorize events they determine as newsworthy, but also their cameras reinforce events through imagery. In Louisville, four television stations present newscasts four times per day, beginning at 6:00 A.M. and ending at 11:00 P.M. Additional three-minute reports appear throughout the day in which short clips advertise upcoming news events. Newscasters are also local celebrities, who appear at charity, sporting, and social events; sometimes, therefore, the news reports on itself. Newscasters themselves are so prominent that a few have run for public office at the state and local level.

This personalization of newscasters reinforces their image as dedicated, objective transmitters of local events. Most important, given the relatively small population of the metropolitan region (less than 1 million residents) and the small budgets of newscasts which restrict the number of times newscasters can be sent out of state to cover nonlocal events, most news is local and repetitious. Therefore, events reported upon tend to become magnified. That is, these news broadcast at 6:00 A.M. is repeated and elaborated upon on subsequent newscasts throughout the day, although when they appear in the broadcast they may change depending upon other "newsbreaking" events.

The local news acts as the primary transmitter of events that take place within African-American neighborhoods and in the lives of African Americans to the larger metropolitan area. The use of the term West End has already been discussed, but here it should be noted that in newscasts one can observe the juxtapositioning of race and place. Indeed, an event may be associated with the West End if it involves an African American. This occurs when events take place in the white working-class enclave of Portland or in other areas of the city that have substantial pockets of African-American residents. For example, when a black grocery store owner was slain in a robbery, the location of the crime site was broadcast as occurring in the West End. Two days passed before the correct site was cited by broadcasters, who substituted "West End" with the appropriate neighborhood, without explanation.

National and local emphasis on crime has acted to demonize African-American communities (Wolf 1994). Local newscasters have deliberately sought to link news occurring in larger metropolitan areas to local events. Such linkages have situated the local within the national in a competitive arena of local broadcasters; broadcasters act as cheerleaders, linking Louisville to larger metropolitan areas such as New York, Atlanta, or Los Angeles. For example, two years ago when the national news "discovered" the existence of African-American gangs in Los Angeles, local newscasters went on a hunting expedition in the city's black neighborhoods. News broadcasters were seen interviewing various African-American youth, questioning them about whether or not they belonged to a gang or knew of any. Finally, they presented a local "gang" to the public and were able to secure an interview with "the leader." This interview with "the gang" and its "leader" took place within a community service organization. Perhaps only the West End residents recognized the "leader" as a Harvard-educated social worker employed as a community outreach worker with the local Urban League.

Similarly, after a "wilding" in New York City's Central Park, local broadcasters attached the same label to black and white youth who were harassing whites, attacking them with sticks and robbing them, which took place in a predominantly white working-class neighborhood. In this instance the "wilding" term was taken up by the print media and criminal justice system which delivered a conviction more appropriate to the situation in New York City than to a disorganized group of youth who were harassing the public.

Local news' emphasis on crime has resulted in the construction of the "West End" as a crime site. Within this context, African Americans are portrayed as criminals, victims of criminal activity, or rehabilitated criminals. The rehabilitated category was constructed for black youth who were organized to clean public streets or alleys, for example, or black youth who participate in after-school tutoring or social service recreational programs. Within this context, African-American adults are portrayed as "rehabilitators."

African-American women are depicted as either dependent upon welfare or demonized mothers who produce criminals or are themselves child abusers. For example, a black mother of twins was arrested for murder when she called the local emergency medical service to report that one of the twins had ceased breathing. Upon arrival, the emergency medical service and police pronounced the baby dead; the police arrested the mother and placed the surviving twin in protective custody. The dilapidated condition of her rented house was instrumental in the authorities' decision to charge her with child abuse and murder.

Even after the medical examiner found that the cause of death was sudden infant death syndrome, the black woman was retained in custody. Subsequently a judge told her that her surviving child would only be released from protective custody when the court was satisfied that the physical environment in which she resided was "cleaned up." The court and public opinion declared this woman an unfit mother, even though she resided in a rented house and was therefore not responsible for the dilapidated conditions of peeling wallpaper and paint, and a leaking roof, conditions for which the owner of the domicile was responsible. This woman disappeared from public view, leaving one to wonder whether she had the resources to make those expensive structural changes or whether or not her landlord would be held accountable. Rather than depict the black woman as a mother who had tragically lost a child, and as a renter dependent on a profit-oriented landlord, the woman was portrayed as an unfit mother.

In addition to the construction of African Americans as criminals, or indirectly associated with crime as victims, rehabilitators, or creating conditions under which future criminal activities will occur, African Americans are portrayed in ritualistic contexts: in church worship services, or as participants in non-Western or "exotic" contexts—Kwanzaa, for example, thereby reinforcing a sense of otherness. Similarly, "otherness" is portrayed as dangerous.

Since the city has only one newspaper, it tends to compete with televised news, functioning to sanction their broadcasts or to add "official" or more elaborate analysis to what is televised, even though in some instances such news articles are placed in the section of the paper designated for local news, or appears alongside obituaries, reinforcing criminality, blackness, and death. More importantly, local broadcasts appear prior to publication in the newspaper. An event occurring at 4:00 P.M. for example, can theoretically appear on the 5:30 and 6:00 evening broadcasts, the 11:00 broadcasts, and the 6:00 A.M. broadcasts the next morning. The item may appear in the morning paper, depending on space, coverage by reporters, and so on. More often it will appear 48 hours after it has been broadcast. It may even occur as a minor event, relegated to a back page when ranked alongside other local, national, or international events. The point is that its appearance at this juncture does not get the public's attention.

THE PRACTICE OF CULTURAL NATIONALISM

In examining the nationalistic character of African-American cultural nationalism, I concentrated on the social organizational dimension (Barth 1966; Firth 1951) of voluntary associations of black Louisvillians: those activities surrounding Kwanzaa which occur within the Christmas season, and the racial discourse of a study group. Both arenas embody nationalistic symbols and African Diaspora connections through time and space to Africans worldwide from a continental center. Most important are the actors of these occasions whose behavior intentionally challenges the subordinate position projected on them in the larger society. Hence, participants are involved in the construction of an African-American identity that allows for a diversity of class position, religious belief, and gender formations, while ritual, practice, and performance milieus draw attention to common descent, shared history and experiences.

The African-American Social Organization

In the newly redecorated basement of a public library located in a working-class neighborhood of Louisville's West End, sixteen adults and one college-aged youth sat around tables placed in a "U" configuration on metal folding chairs. Two rooms in the library basement had recently been renovated, decorated with African cloth, sculpture and musical instruments and furnished with $15,000 worth of books (fiction and nonfiction) for children, thanks to a donation from a local politician. It was 6:00 P.M. on a warm July Monday, and some of the seventeen participants walked to the library from their homes, although the overwhelming majority appeared in cars, having driven directly from work. A podium was placed in the center of the tables. A small, middle-aged black woman, a recent graduate of a local but nationally known seminary, was engaged in conversation. The mood was casual, relaxed. There was little conversation between those in the room. Periodically, we were joined by another participant. At approximately 6:30 P.M., the woman took her place at the podium and announced that the meeting was to begin.

After extending greetings to those present, the woman, an ordained Baptist minister and Associate Pastor of a church, led the group in prayer. The following events then occurred. (1) Guests, potential members, and members whose attendance was sporadic were formally greeted or introduced. (2) Countries on the African continent were recited in unison, including the island countries located off its Indian and Atlantic Ocean coasts. This recitation was done by region, beginning with those located in the west, followed by countries bordering the Mediterranean, followed by Egypt, the Sudan, and Ethiopia, the countries of the east and then southern and central Africa. Coastal islands were cited last. Sometimes this was repeated, depending upon the memories of those present. (3) Announcements of upcoming community events were shared. (4) News relevant to the African continent was cited and discussed. Some participants brought news articles that had been published in local or national newspapers or magazines. Over the two years in which I participated as a member, these articles ranged from political events to distinctive cultural practices, but information which focused on archaeological or historical topics was especially welcome and extensively commented upon. These included any articles which focused on early man in Africa, the uncovering of sites of archaeological significance, the ancient history of Africa, and items appearing on ancient Egyptian civilization. (5) The formal segment of the meeting began when everyone's attention turned to a black male, who proceeded to summarize a few chapters of a text written by the now deceased black historian Leo Hansberry, an early pioneer in advocating the study of African history. Most participants followed the discussion using texts they obtained in their library research, and they took notes. Those without texts looked on with those who did. Often someone cited information gleaned from another text, and sometimes a new text was passed around. One male member regularly appeared at meetings with several texts, notes, and xeroxed articles that he passed around and discussed. Participants often argued over the interpretation of data or challenged each other for accuracy. This segment of the meeting frequently lasted two hours, but the group leader, standing at the podium, set the meeting's tempo, either by calling on another person or stating that time was passing. (6) The meeting was formally closed between 8:30 and 9:00 P.M. The assignment for the following week was discussed, and often announcements cited earlier would be repeated.

The preceding describes in brief the social organization of the Louisville chapter of a national organization developed by two black males in California approximately five years ago in order to inspire interest in ancient and modern Africa at the grass-roots level. There are approximately twenty chapters throughout the United States. Chapters can be set up simply by requesting a charter from the home organization, and dues are $35 annually, shared between the local chapter and the national organization. Each chapter elects a slate of officers, a president, a treasurer, and an events coordinator. Other positions may be created if necessary. The national chapter also provides a list of recommended texts to be discussed, although it is up to each chapter to construct its own curriculum. Texts can be deleted or added, so that great variation exists between one chapter and another.

Membership in the Louisville chapter fluctuated between thirty-five and sixty dues-paying members over the course of my two-year period of active participation. Meetings had an average attendance of sixteen, but as many as sixty people might appear at a special event. Membership consisted primarily of middle-aged, working-class African Americans. Parents often brought their high school-age children with them to meetings. At the meeting described above, attendance included, in addition to the ordained minister, the Associate Pastor of a Baptist church, a seminary student, a retired worker of the city's bureaucracy who was currently studying Hebrew at a local seminary, two postal workers, an employee of a local university, a restaurant worker, three unemployed persons, and two staff persons of a local hospital.

Members were recruited through both word of mouth and an ad periodically placed in the local newspaper, which probably accounted for the range of occupations and backgrounds. During my two-year period of active membership, the organization sponsored three special events. It hosted a regional meeting of the national organization in which two national officers attended. Organized as a one-day conference held in the auditorium of a local high school on a Saturday, the conference featured a keynote address presented by a local scholar and John Henrick Clark, Professor Emeritus, Hunter College, who, together with his assistant, were flown in for the event. The conference also featured a luncheon catered by a local restaurant, as the school's cafeteria was closed. Participants paid a $20 conference fee, and the event attracted approximately sixty people. The second event was a Kwanzaa celebration, held during the Christmas holidays. This event was free, took place in the library basement and attracted over one hundred participants. This Kwanzaa also featured a guest speaker who delivered a "keynote" address, a student who recited poetry, a musical recitation, and an African drum group consisting of adolescent males. The third event took place in the "party room" of a local restaurant. Approximately twenty persons attended after paying a $5 fee. In this event a retired black female professor from a nearby university presented a lecture/slide show on ancient Egyptian civilization, after which participants had lunch in the restaurant.

This voluntary association, similar in function to the study groups organized by the urban Chinese in the late 19th century, arose largely in response to Western contact and internal disruption (Dikotter 1992). It also has its place in African-American tradition, for groups similar in purpose were operated throughout the North by free blacks during the ante-bellum era (although with a decidedly Western focus and orientation), by black women's social uplift clubs beginning earlier in this century (Giddings 1984), and in cities throughout the country during the Harlem Renaissance (Lewis 1981). The Louisville study group functions primarily to stimulate interest in African history, but it is also concerned with "uncovering truths" about the primacy of Africa in the development of humankind and situating Egyptian civilization firmly in Africa. The texts utilized were written by W.E.B. Du Bois, John H. Clarke, Carter G. Woodson, J. A. Rogers (whose works were privately published and sold on the street corners of Harlem when I was a child) and Cheikh Anta Diop (1991). These scholars were largely published in the 1920s and 1930s. Their works did not constitute mainstream scholarship at the time, and so they remained unrecognized. Of these works, Diop's *Civilization or Barbarism: An Authentic Anthropology* is held in high esteem as *Ancient Civilizations of Africa* edited by G. Mokhatar (1981), volume two of six in a series of texts on African history. The publication series was the result of an international effort of historians residing primarily in Africa, but it also included participants from Singapore, Portugal, the former USSR and the former Federal Republic of Germany. Scholars from NATO nations were notably absent. Difficult to find, this publication was copied and passed around by members.

Within this context, most of the texts focused upon were Pan African in context, although the texts themselves were never discussed as constituting a specific theoretical focus, were never examined for methodological approaches, and scant attention was paid to distinctions between primary and secondary sources, or lines of inquiry leading to other areas of investigation. Instead, texts were read as truths, part of a hidden history. Authors were venerated as one would esteemed or deceased ancestor-scholars who struggled under oppressive conditions to uncover truths masked by centuries of Western domination. This belief was reinforced by the difficulty encountered in acquiring the texts. Most were out of print and could no longer be ordered through bookstores, or they were listed as "lost" in public libraries. Some texts were reprints of earlier editions or were privately published. Text authors were drawn from the periphery of educational institutions, laboring in black colleges or teaching in public schools. Many were no longer living. Members practiced uncovering truth and restoring the glory of individuals and the race. Texts were central to this objective, and their general unavailability contributed to their sacredness.

The appearance of John Henrik Clarke at the organization's regional conference illuminated the juxtapositioning of ancestral veneration, history, and scholarship. Dr. Clarke, who is now blind and in his 80s, attended the conference with his attendant. He was paid a small stipend and the chapter covered his travel and hotel expenses through dues and donations. His plane was late, and he arrived shortly before the luncheon; after a period of repose, he gave some introductory remarks before the luncheon. Dr. Clarke's remarks were drawn from his own personal history, in which he wove his life events into the major trajectories of the African Diaspora in the 20th century: Nkrumah and the West African Independence Movement, W.E.B. Du Bois and his attendance at Pan African Congress meetings, and Marcus Garvey. European authors who gave primacy to ancient African civilizations were also cited. His voice was soft spoken and his body was frail with age, but his very presence bespoke strength, a triumph. His dark glasses and the presence of his attendant added a distant, mystical quality to his persona. He was treated with reverence and consideration, and he, in turn was not distant but easily mixed with those present, conversing.

The activities of the study group are similar to those of other historically focused voluntary associations organized by Louisville's African Americans. During my period of active membership, I became aware of seven such organizations: two were held in public housing projects on Saturday mornings, one was organized as part of the ministry of an Afrocentric Baptist Church, and another was attached to a black Lutheran congregation. Three defined themselves as book clubs. All collected membership dues, organized or participated in cultural and scholarly events, and read similar texts. Participants were predominantly middle age, although the retired constituted a significant percentage of participants, upwards to 20%. Participants had, on the whole, working- or middle-class occupations and incomes. These organizations did not have any structural linkages between them, nor did they have overlapping memberships, although the book clubs did constitute friendship networks.

Kwanzaa

I arrived at the entrance of a community center located in one of the city's most "demonized" public housing projects at 6:30 P.M. one evening, four days after Christmas. The center was adjacent to a well-lit parking lot, full of cars and people, who were joined by people who arrived on foot. Their formal attire, including several women and children in African dress, and the quiet casualness of their demeanor, formed a sharp reality with the image of the housing project and its occupants constructed by the local media. I had come to participate in the celebration of "Ujamaa," cooperative economics; this is the main principle delineated on the fourth day of Kwanzaa, a seven-day period of cultural observance.

After entering the building I followed the crowd into a large cafeteria located on the first floor. Metal folding chairs had been placed in a semicircle facing the rear of the room. A podium was situated at the apex, next to a long narrow table. Participants were directed to a small adjacent room reserved for coats. After greeting people and hanging up my coat, I joined a nearby group of participants and obtained a program of the evening's events. There were perhaps a hundred and twenty people in attendance, twenty were young girls ranging from the ages of 3 through 12 years in identical African dress, members of a local dance troupe. Perhaps three-fourths of the participants were women and children, residents of the housing project.

While most people conversed with one another, several women were arranging items on a table adjacent to the podium. They covered the table with several cloths of African design, and bowls of fruits and vegetables; they also placed several small African artifacts on placemats (two statues and a small drum), and a large bowl of fresh ears of corn on the table. On the table's center, the women placed a seven-branched candleholder, a large cup, bottle of wine, several wrapped Christmas gifts, and seven large red and green candles. They then directed their attention to arranging three long tables, which they placed along one side of the room.

Approximately 45 minutes after my arrival, a middle-aged man dressed in African fashion went to the podium and asked everyone to be seated. The dance troupe and other children sat on the floor in front of the adults. Due to the placement of the chairs, people were sitting in a semicircle around whomever would be speaking from the podium. While a loudspeaker was available, none was needed due to the intimacy of the seating arrangement. After the man had everyone's attention, he introduced himself as one member of a local voluntary association who was sponsoring the Kwanzaa ceremony that evening. A former "radical/activist" during the 1960s he had been employed by a number of community outreach programs that target the housing project, and he was well known to most of those present. Acting as a master of ceremonies, he then directed the Kwanzaa ceremony. A brief outline of that event follows:

> a. "Elders! Do we have permission to speak?" This question served to formally announce the opening of the ceremony and to signal its Diaspora quality. He then explained that it is an African tradition to request permission to speak when one's elders are in the room.

b. Introduction of distinguished guests and elders; two ministers stood and were recognized, as was a former civil rights activist, now in his 80s who was instrumental in undertaking a lawsuit that resulted in the integration of state–supported colleges and universities.
c. A Christian prayer was presented by one of the ministers.
d. The dance troupe of girls performed a dance to traditional African music played on a small cassette player.
e. Introduction of guest speaker and presentation. The speaker was a retired school teacher who was active in local Democratic party activities, and had been appointed to several city and state commissions in the past. The text of his presentation fit the theme of the evening— "Ujamaa,"— cooperative economics—and he spoke on the virtues of achieving racial self–sufficiency through education and entrepreneurship.
f. Shortly after this presentation, approximately eighteen young black males entered the room still wearing their winter outerwear and carrying several large musical instruments. After getting the attention of the master of ceremonies, they were escorted to the coatroom. We were then told that these males were members of an African-inspired music band from Cincinnati who had driven some 90 miles to perform. The master of ceremonies told us that they had tried to arrive sooner but were unexpectedly delayed. We were then urged to welcome their appearance, and as they left the coatroom and reentered the cafeteria they were greeted with enthusiastic applause.
g. The band, consisting of twelve active players utilizing at least seven musical instruments ranging from drums and electrical guitars to tambourines performed three pieces to an enthusiastic and appreciative audience.
h. A woman sitting in the audience rose and walked to the front of the room, situating herself in the middle of the table; I recognized her as one of the women who arranged the articles on the table earlier that evening. After introducing herself, she stated that her intention was to preside over the "Kuchangilia," or rejoicing part of the ceremony. She began by reciting the seven principles of Kwanzaa, and she asked the audience to repeat each principle. Soon after, I noticed that seven women approached the front of the room; each one held up a large poster containing a principle written in Swahili and English and its meaning. After first presenting a history of the ceremony, she then explained that the length of the ceremony, seven days, corresponded with the number of principles. She began to list and explain each principle and asked the audience to repeat after her, in unison. Women with the appropriate posters stepped forward in turn to assist the audience with its task. The woman then explained the significance of the items placed on the table. Corn, it was explained, represented the children in the audience, the fruits and vegetables stood for unified effort, and the straw mats, tradition. The cup was termed "KiKombe cha umoja"—a communal cup for libations. The gifts wrapped in Christmas paper symbolized educational toys, the seven-branch candleholder, the "kinara," symbolized the African continent, and each candle symbolized one of the seven principles of Kwanzaa. The woman then placed the candles in the candleholders and lit the first four candles. She poured some wine in the communal cup, placed

it down on the table, and announced that now was the time to call out the names of deceased family members, African and African-American heroes and historic figures, or the names of persons we had lost contact with. The audience responded in unison to the accompaniment of drums.
i. The master of ceremonies returned to the podium. He introduced the last formal event of the evening, a youngster who presented a series of poems, but no one was listening. It was almost 9:30 and the children were beginning to stand up and walk around. Some took the opportunity to leave the building to smoke a cigarette.
j. The master of ceremonies reappeared at the podium. He asked everyone to stand and stretch, and then he asked that everyone to move their chairs back against the wall. While this was being done, several of the male band members appeared with a large package that they proceeded to unwrap in the middle of the room. We were told that it was a parachute, made out of the strongest fabric available. We were then asked to stand in a circle, and each person was to assist in holding up the parachute. All the children in the room were then asked to form a line. Each child in turn walked across the parachute to the opposite side while it was held up by the adult participants. The entire exercise would illustrate the African proverb: it takes an entire village to raise a child. As adult participants held up their section of the parachute, they were challenged to bear the weight of the child, as well as account for the frailties of persons standing adjacent to them.

Preschoolers were coaxed to "walk the parachute" first, followed by children of grammar school age. They were challenged to stand up straight and not fall down. Adults holding up the parachute strained under their weight, as the children, one by one, walked hesitantly, their bodies tight with anxiety, and then straight with confidence, negotiated the parameters of the fabric. Their efforts were rewarded by the adults, who shouted words of encouragement, their laughter and groans contributing to the merriment of the event. This unified effort lasted some 45 minutes and its ending signaled the conclusion of the Kwanzaa ritual.

k. The master of ceremonies returned to the podium and announced that the Kwanzaa was over. He then announced that everyone was invited to eat. At that point, several men, women, and children appeared from the kitchen section of the cafeteria. Each held dishes of food, which they then placed on the table. A group of adolescent females brought out paper plates, napkins, and cutlery. People then stood in line to await their turn at the food tables while others huddled in conversation.

According to a recent news article, over 12 million African Americans celebrated Kwanzaa in 1993. Originally conceived by Ron Karenga, a university professor and founder of US, a cultural nationalist movement centered in California in the 1960s, the celebration seeks to preserve unity and an appreciation of an African Diaspora history and culture. Many of the terms used in the ceremony, the seven principles, the objects placed on the table, and the program text are presented in Swahili which Karenga purposely chose for its Diaspora features. Since its first celebration in 1966, I have witnessed its growth in Louisville over a period of two decades.

I was able to find blacks in Louisville who had been celebrating Kwanzaa since the 1970s. Early participants were young, in their early 20s. During these early years, they tended to celebrate with friends, leaving Christmas celebrations for family occasions. Many continued the practice after beginning their own families. Some participated only sporadically, while a few diligently attended all seven nights of the celebration. One informant's experience with Kwanzaa illustrates its early formation and growth. Mr. and Mrs. Banks were both born and raised in Louisville. After graduating from college, Mr. Banks secured a position as a social worker at the YMCA in a city in New Jersey. He participated in his first Kwanzaa while on a site business in Michigan in the early 1970s. Participants were distributing instructions on the ceremony and he took one back with him when he returned to New Jersey. A growing family and financial restraints made the Banks decide to substitute Kwanzaa one Christmas season, which he said was successful due in part to the ages of their children, who were excited by the changes and the length of the celebration. After he saw how well it worked, he convinced the YMCA to utilize it in its annual Christmas program. News of the celebration traveled through organizational newsletters and the next year they received inquiries from other YMCAs around the country asking for instructions. Despite a fear of reprisals from white administrators, Mr. Banks and another black colleague decided to submit the instructions to the national newsletter where it would be widely distributed.

Concurrently, Mrs. Banks was making changes at home, and the following year she decided to make the Kwanzaa ceremony a community-wide event. At first, they invited the children from the neighborhood, after carefully securing permission from their parents. A few years after that parents were included. Over the next fifteen years Mr. Banks's position at the YMCA took them to several cities in the East and Midwest. Over time, Kwanzaa became a permanent substitute for Christmas, attended by their children's friends and neighbors. After Mr. Banks retired, they moved back to Louisville after an absence of more than twenty years. Mrs. Banks is known as a Kwanzaa resource person. She has two large suitcases containing Kwanzaa ceremonial items and African artifacts which she takes with her to different Kwanzaa ceremonies. She directs the "Kuchangilia" or rejoicing segment of the ceremony, and conducts entire Kwanzaa ceremonies in the public schools when requested.

The "Ujamaa" Kwanzaa ceremony was one of seven countywide ceremonies constituting a Kwanzaa network held during the Christmas season of 1993. The network was organized by ten women for the purpose of coordinating and publicizing the African-inspired harvest festival. The group published and distributed a free directory listing all Kwanzaa events, times, and places during the seven day duration of the celebration period. Their objectives were to promote the principles of Kwanzaa and speed its growth. The Kwanzaa activities listed were sponsored by a variety of churches and voluntary associations and were held at a number of sites, ranging from church recreation centers to neighborhood libraries.

While Karenga developed the text for the holiday, my participation in several Kwanzaas in Louisville over a five-year period yielded some variation in practice. One was the degree to which Christian theology entered the Kwanzaa ceremony. Although this was largely dependent on the nature of the sponsoring organization and the master of ceremonies, more than once I heard loud objections over the insertion of Christian prayer and other references to Christianity in the ceremonies. Some Kwanzaas I attended set aside a special time during the ceremony during which individual participants were encouraged to air grievances or to reconcile with family members. After individuals participated, the master of ceremonies cited some aspect of their slave history in order to account for their present difficulties. One participant, for example, stated that she felt estranged from her sisters and wondered whether it was due to her dark complexion. Other participants spoke of the competition between slaves on plantations and the separation of "house" and "field" slaves. Another person asked whether or not this aspect of slavery was really true, which resulted in a general discussion of slavery, lasting some 40 minutes of heated debate.

ENTREPRENEURSHIP AND THE COMMODIFICATION OF AFRICA

The magnification of events such as those described above has yielded a market in Afrocentric merchandise in Louisville, Kentucky. Central to this emerging pattern of African-American entrepreneurship is the Kwanzaa principle of Ujamaa. Afrocentric merchants are primarily vendors, traveling in a six-state circuit from one black convention to another with their merchandise: books, posters, prints, fabric, jewelry, and sometimes African sculpture and basketry, as well as Afrocentric Christmas and Kwanzaa cards and stationery. The more successful vendors become store owners and may utilize vendor strategies less often as their businesses become established. In 1995 there were twelve black-owned Afrocentric businesses in Louisville, five of which are located in predominantly white suburban areas, catering to a more affluent clientele who may be interested in purchasing articles for interior decoration or to accessorize an outfit.

I became more familiar with another store, however, located in a newly constructed mall in Louisville's West End. *The African Griot* dominated the local Afrocentric marketing niche, drawing African Americans from throughout the city and metropolitan area. In business at the site since 1992, the company was founded by a married couple and their two male friends. Their store features clothing, art, and books and has the largest selection of books authored by African Americans and related topics in the metropolitan area. Their success resulted in a downtown bookstore, which was part of a national franchise, stocking a large collection of books of interest to African-American readers and displaying them prominently. Suburban bookstores soon followed this marketing strategy.

The African Griot began as a circuit vending operation in the mid-1980s. After three years they purchased their first store, in Nashville, Tennessee. At present they have expanded, opening stores in Cincinnati, Ohio and St. Louis, Missouri. In addition to offering merchandise for sale, they have noted autograph parties for nationally recognized African-American authors and have sponsored Kwanzaa celebrations at their store.

Similarly, another Afrocentric enterprise is the *Sahara Cafe*, the metropolitan area's only restaurant featuring African, Caribbean, and African-American cuisine. This business venture was formed through the joint efforts of three individuals who met as members of a city-sponsored Sister Cities organization, an international organization that pairs U.S. cities with other cities throughout the world. In addition to communicating with their counterparts in other cities through mail and cassette tapes, the organization sponsors exchanges between visiting delegations of adults and students. The owners of the Cafe, an African-American male elected official, a white professor of African history and a Ghanian airline pilot, deliberately chose a downtown location, a central place where "East meets West," as one of the owners informed me, clearly referring to the racial and geographic distance of the city. The *Cafe* has also sponsored Kwanzaa ceremonies and is a frequent meeting place for numerous voluntary organizations. Its Ethiopian staff reinforces the African atmosphere of the restaurant.

Both the *Cafe* and the apparel/bookstore market culture as well as merchandise firms recognize that an educational awareness of Africa can increase the stability of their enterprises in the long run. The *Cafe*, for example, features a reggae band one evening per week and has conducted lectures and slide presentations on different topics relevant to the African continent for their patrons. Artistic works focusing on African themes decorate the walls of the restaurant, and many are offered for sale. Their marketing strategy of "East meets West," however, has been more successful during weekdays than on evenings and weekends, when the downtown is generally empty of pedestrian traffic.

Before concluding our examination of the social and commercial arenas in which cultural nationalism is practiced, let us focus on one more example of enterprising behavior in which a particular religious ideology is central to the principles expressed in "Ujamaa." Upon attending a Career Fair for students held at a local high school one Sunday, I was introduced to one of the organizers, a middle-aged black woman dressed in conservative Western attire. The Fair was sponsored by a voluntary association of black female Muslims interested in embarking on a number of entrepreneurial ventures. In organizing the Career Fair, they hoped to merge these commercial objectives with educational and career information, and they had been successful in persuading several local corporations and colleges to send their representatives to the event. The Fair was held in the school's cafeteria and was divided into two areas of activity. On one side of the room, black and white corporate and educational representatives sat at tables filled with information on their respective corporations or schools. At the other half of the room, divided by a large screen, sat members of the voluntary association at tables on which a wide variety of items were for sale. In addition to the art, jewelry, greeting cards and books I observed at previous events, cosmetics, "vitamins," shampoos, perfumes and a variety of oils for the bath and body were featured, all sold under labels I did not recognize. When I inquired as to whether these articles were available locally in retail stores, I was told that they were manufactured and distributed by association members. In conversations with members, each stressed that their products were free of chemicals and other impurities, unlike, I was informed, similar products available at retail outlets. While stressing the uniqueness of their products, their items for sale also symbolized racial uplift, solidarity, and cooperation, economic productivity and autonomy, values embodied in their Muslim sisterhood. Organizing the Career Fair enabled the members to "practice what is preached" in their religious tenants.

CONCLUSIONS

As we have seen, a significant and increasing percentage of African Americans residing in a midsize city of the Upper South, following a national pattern, has sought to emphasize their African identify through periodic participation in educational and ritualistic activities. In contrast, the city's white-controlled visual and print media construct the African-American communities in their midst, depicting blacks as criminals, victims of criminal behavior, rehabilitated criminals, and unfit mothers producing more of the same. The Afrocentric practices presented here challenge this hegemony. While each local broadcast station covers at least one Kwanzaa celebration during the winter holiday season and the city's one newspaper will display at least one color photograph of a child participant, perhaps even on the front page, the activities presented here are largely invisible to the wider society. The first mention of Kwanzaa in the city's newspaper occurred in 1991, almost twenty years after it began to be observed in large numbers locally. This should remind us that while the media are central to domestic culture and can penetrate more deeply into the "receiving culture" than any previous manifestation of Western technology (Said 1994), in minority or marginalized communities, they report "partial truths" and hence they construct images that are challenged in other social contexts.

Obviously, these cultural practices can be analyzed on several levels. Twenty years ago, these activities might have been viewed through the lens of adaptive strategies. At another, more individualistic level, participants embodied a "culture of achievement" similar to the low-income mothers of New York City's Head Start programs examined by Delmos Jones (1993).

An examination of the items that are displayed and sold, however, together with the ritualistic arenas in which these transactions take place, allows us to view these practices as specifically related to the construction of a transnational identity. The commodities focused on in this chapter illuminate the Diaspora nature of an African identity, incorporating the dimensions of both time and space. For example, the lithographs, greeting cards, original paintings, and posters overwhelmingly depict family scenes in which males are present and are extended and multigenerational, in settings that could be African or rural America, Harlem or Accra. Jewelry items and sculpture ranged from those that drew on ancient Egypt in design to items obtained from Brazil and Zimbabwe. Books were viewed as sacred texts, and in the case of the Afrocentric study group, represented lost and subjugated knowledge that was to be shared and distributed rather than purchased. In this light, Kwanzaa festivals became contexts through which these Afrocentric items were ritualized and given meaning. Equally important is the wearing of African dress by those offering these commodities, the taking of African or Afrocentric names, and the production of cosmetics free of impurities for the uniqueness of women of African descent. The commodities focused on in this chapter, as well as the ritualized Diaspora contexts analyzed, are to be found in large and small cities throughout this country, and participants represent a cross section of the African-American population.

Together with the playing of reggae music from the Caribbean, and breakdancing, which is Afro-Brazilian in origin and other items of black popular culture, these commodities circulate throughout the Atlantic community of Africans, linking the populations of four continents through time and space (Gilroy 1993). Unlike the Pan Africanist nationalism of the 19th and 20th centuries, which was concerned with eliminating colonialism and acquiring citizenship status, the diasporic and Afrocentric practices described here represent the emergence of nationalistic aspirations and identities which cross-cut political boundaries and are not concerned with a separate and national political culture. On the contrary, this transnationalism unites Latino, Anglo, Christian, Muslim, and other hybrid African cultures, while minimizing conflicts of gender and class. Indeed, I once witnessed a symposium in which the participants—all black—disagreed strongly over the role of women in society. The atmosphere was infused with anger as the feminists present were accused of "selling out." However, after the symposium, participants left the hotel conference room to patronize vendors selling their Afrocentric goods.

This new Diaspora transnationalism embraces the ideals of racial solidarity, and a recognition of Africa as a homeland, fosters belief in a distinct African personality, and has as its objective the restoration of Africa's history, ideals, and objectives shared by the Kwanzaa and study group participants profiled in this chapter. The golden age of black nationalism occurred between 1850 and 1925. This era encompassed slavery, emancipation, return migration to parts of West Africa, colonialism, and one world war. Involved Africans of the Diaspora ranged from Marcus Garvey to Alexander Crumwell and W.E.B. Du Bois, each defining and offering an alternative to domination.

Although this chapter linked a specific pattern of black entrepreneurship to cultural nationalism, generating a market emerging from its cultural center, this trend is taking place within a larger pattern of black cultural commodification and appropriation by middle-class white youth (hooks 1992). Correspondingly, middle-class African Americans are beginning to question the values and objectives of assimilation and acculturation as never before (Early 1993). Perhaps the viability of this pattern of entrepreneurship will reflect the viability of cultural autonomy among African Americans.

The segregated location of blacks in Louisville to the West End physically defines or outlines their community. According to Warren (1978:9), community is "that combination of social units and systems that perform the major social functions having locality relevance." Community is both geographic and psychologic. Geographically, it identifies a cluster of individuals, while psychologically it indicates shared interests, shared social characteristics, and social interaction. Frequency and intensity of interaction and segregation of association are the main ingredients determining community identity (Hillery 1955; Hutchinson et al. 1996; Warren 1978). The history of Louisville and the state of Kentucky situated in the South, and the legacy of this history for race relations, influences black Louisvillians' sense of community and ethnic identity. There is a comaraderie and shared sense of identity in response to the negativism of white Louisvillians. This sense of racial identity is partially a reaction to the legacy of slavery and the negativism associated with race relations in the South.

The celebration of Kwanzaa, the voluntary study groups, and the proliferation of Afrocentric entrepreneurs are also responses to negative images of African Americans created by white Americans following the transportation of dark-skinned people to the New World. Knowing that such stereotypes are not representative of African Americans, black Louisvillians sought to develop their own racial identity by covering their "true past" and by economically capitalizing on this past. This is not a negative, but a positive development of racial identity among people inundated with negative images and stereotypes of themselves. In conclusion, the segregated location of blacks in Louisville and the development of Afrocentric celebrations, study groups, and entrepreneurs are producing a positive image of African Americans. It is allowing them to develop a racial identity devoid of the negative images and connotations of white America.

REFERENCES

Asante, M.K. 1980. *Afrocentricity: The Theory of Social Change*. Buffalo, N.Y.: Amulefi Publishing Co.
———. 1988. *The Afrocentric Idea*. Philadelphia: Temple University Press.
Barth, F. 1966. *Models of Social Organization*. London: Royal Anthropological Institute.
Branch, T. 1988. *Parting the Waters: America During the King Years, 1954–1963*. New York: Simon and Schuster.
Brown, E. 1993. *Taste of Power: A Black Woman's Story*. New York: Pantheon Books.
Carson, C. 1981. *In the Struggle*. Cambridge, Mass.: Harvard University Press.

Cole, J. 1985. Africanisms in the Americas: A Brief History of the Concept. *Anthropology and Humanism Quarterly* 10 (4): 120–126.

Dikotter, F. 1992. *The Discourse of Race in Modern China*. Stanford, Calif.: Stanford University Press.

Diop, C. A. 1991. *Civilization or Barbarism: An Authentic Anthropology*. New York: Lawrence Hill Books.

Drake, St. C. and Clayton, H. 1945. *Black Metropolis: A Study of Negro Life in a Northern City*. Chicago: University of Chicago Press.

Early, G. 1993. *Lure and Loathing: Essays on Race, Identity and the Ambivalence of Assimilation*. New York: Allen Lane

Fine, E. H. 1973. *The African American Artist*. New York: Holt, Rhinehart and Winston.

Firth, R. 1951. *Elements of Social Organization*. London: Watts.

Garrow, D. 1988. *Bearing the Cross*. New York: Vintage.

Giddings, P. 1984. *When and Where I Enter: The Impact of Black Women on Race and Sex in America*. New York: William Morrow.

Gilroy, P. 1993. *The Black Atlantic: Modernity and Double Consciousness*. Cambridge, Mass.: Harvard University Press.

Hamilton, C. and Carmichael, S. 1967. *Black Power: The Politics of Liberation in America*. New York: Random House.

Harvey, P. 1993. From Space to Place and Back Again: Reflections On the Condition of Post Modernity. In J. Bird, B. Curtis et al., eds., *Mapping the Future*. New York: Routledge.

Hazzard-Gordon, K. 1990. *Jookin': The Rise of Social Dance Formations in African American Culture*. Philadelphia: Temple University Press.

Hillery, G.A. 1955. Definitions of Community: Areas of Agreement. *Rural Sociology* 20(2): 111–123.

hooks, b. 1992. *Race and Representation*. Boston: South End Press.

Hutchinson, J., Rodriguez, N. and Hagan J. 1996. Community Life: African Americans in Multi-Ethnic Residential Areas. *Journal of Black Studies* 27(2): 201–223.

Jones, D. 1993. The Culture of Achievement Among the Poor: The Case of Mothers and Children in a Head Start Program. *Critique* 13(3): 247–266.

Karenga, M. 1993. *Introduction to Black Studies*. Los Angeles, Calif.: University of Sankore Press.

Kasinitz, P. 1992. *Caribbean New York: Black Immigration and the Politics of Race*. Ithaca: Cornell University Press.

Laguerre, M. 1984. *American Odyssey: Haitians in New York City*. Ithaca, N.Y.: Cornell University Press.

Lefkowitz, M. 1996. *Not Out of Africa: How Afrocentrism Became an Excuse to Teach Myth as History*. New York: Basic Books.

Lefkowitz, M. and Rogers, G. eds. 1995. *Black Athena Revisted*. Chapel Hill: University of North Carolina Press.

Lewis, D. L. 1981. *When Harlem Was In Vogue*. New York: Alfred Knopf.

Mahaniah, K.1982. The Presence of Black Americans in the Lower Congo, 1878–1921. In J.E. Harris, ed., *Global Dimensions of the African Diaspora*. Washington, D.C.: Howard University Press. pp. 405–420.

Marable, M. and Mullings, L. 1994. The Divided Mind of Black America: Race, Ideology and Politics in the Post Civil Rights Era. *Race and Class* 35(1): 61–72

Mokhatar, G., ed. 1981. *Ancient Civilizations of Africa. General History of Africa.* Berkeley: University of California Press.
Morrison, T. 1987. *Beloved.* New York: Alfred Knopf.
Naylor, G. 1983. *The Women of Brewster Place.* New York: Viking Penguin.
Osofsky, G. 1966. *Harlem, the Making of a Ghetto: Negro New York 1890–1930.* New York: Harper and Row.
Phiri, K. 1982. Afro-American Influence in Colonial Malawi, 1891–1945. In J.E. Harris, ed., *Global Dimensions of the African Diaspora.* Washington, D.C: Howard University Press, pp. 387–404.
Portes, A. 1994. *City on the Edge: The Transformation of Miami.* Berkeley: University of California Press.
Said, E. 1994. *Culture and Imperialism.* New York: Alfred Knopf.
Stowe, H. 1970. *Uncle Tom's Cabin.* New York: Harper Collins (originally published 1852).
Sutton, C. R. and Chaney, E., eds. 1987. *Caribbean Life in New York: Sociocultural Dimensions.* New York: Center for Migration Studies.
Van Sertima, I. 1976. *They Came Before Columbus.* New York: Random House.
———. 1985a. *African Presence in Early Asia.* New Brunswick, N.J.: Transaction Press.
———. 1985b. *African Presence in Early Europe.* New Brunswick, N.J.: Transaction Press.
Warren, R.L. 1978. *The Community in America.* Lanham, Md.: University Press of America.
Williams, W. 1982. *Black Americans and the Evangelization of Africa.* Madison: University of Wisconsin Press.
Wolf, E. 1994. Perilous Ideas: Race, Culture, People. *Current Anthropology* 35(1): 1–12.
Wright, G. 1985. *Life Behind the Veil: Blacks in Louisville, Kentucky.* Baton Rouge: Louisiana State University Press.
———. 1990. *Racial Violence in Kentucky.* Baton Rouge: Louisiana State University Press.

CHAPTER 7

Creating a Racial Identity
Janis Faye Hutchinson

The contributors to this volume provide diverse portrayals of African Americans in America. Americans and the world population are aware of the social problems faced by African Americans, especially, the high rates of teenage pregnancy, female-headed households, unemployment, poverty, alcoholism, criminal victimization and drug addiction (Oliver 1989; Poussaint 1983). Less well known is the fact that these groups are a minority within a minority. That is, such individuals are a small segment of the group rather than a representation of the group. Like all other racial/ethnic groups, African Americans are a heterogeneous population. However, the media, social and biological scientists, and the majority population study and interact with blacks as if they are a homogeneous group that can be reduced to a single variable, race. As a result, African Americans have a uniformly negative image. The uniformity of negativism comes from portrayals of African Americans by the majority white population. Historically, the whites' desire for political and economic privilege formed the basis for prejudice, discrimination, and racism toward African-derived people. Racist, negative, and uniform images of African Americans were created to justify historical and contemporary racism. Today, we still live with the legacy of historical racism. As a result, negative portrayals of African Americans continue to be perpetuated in popular and scientific forums.

At the eighty-eighth annual meeting of the American Anthropological Association (1989), Eric Wolf, the distinguished lecturer, discussed structural power, a mode of power that is "power that not only operates within settings of domains, but that also organizes and orchestrates the settings themselves, and that specifies the distribution and direction of energy flows" (Wolf 1990:586). According to Wolf, this is the type of power that Foucault believed structured "the possible field of action of others" (Foucault 1984:428). It is this type of structural power that the second and third chapters address. Both focus on the power that the majority population, through its scientists and media, have in creating negative stereotypes about blacks and the maintenance of those negative stereotypes. The majority population organizes and orchestrates the scientific setting and the media. They decide what news is important and how information is to be distributed and directed. Racism is an integral component in the production of scientific knowledge. Scientists generate hypotheses, decide who to test it on, develop methods for data collection, and interpret their findings based on their sociocultural upbringing. When research orientations and findings are reported, this aspect of the scientific process is seldom discussed. If the methods are appropriate, then results are considered valid until another reasonable study contradicts it. What is considered scientific is determined by the dominant European-derived group in America. Although this group has a long history of maintaining prejudice, discrimination, and racism in America, it seldom examines itself and its motivation for conducting scientific inquiry. Given the existence of racism in the United States, how can whites objectively study dark-skinned people? It seems to be assumed that if "scientists" decide to study something, it must be a worthwhile endeavor; anyone who objects is considered emotional and nonscientific. Such accusations are attempts to maintain stereotypes of people of color, denying a voice to activist scientists, and to maintain privilege for the dominant scientific group.

The chapters on biological hypotheses and the media examine the motivation of non-African-American interpretations of the behavior and culture of blacks. They provide an historical perspective which shows that "new racist ideas have evolved all the way from classical antiquity, utilizing the images of medieval thought and the colour symbolisms of Christianity to inform discriminatory practice right into the modern period" (Allahar 1993:52). Oliver (1989) pointed out that the etiology of the aforementioned social problems among African Americans is divided into three positions: genetic inferiority, culture of poverty, or racial oppression. Believers in the genetic inferiority argument stress that genes are the cause of criminality and other antisocial behavior. That these factors are problems in the African-American community means that the problems are genetically or racially based and therefore unsolvable from a social perspective. Oliver (1989) points out a major problem associated with theories of genetic inferiority is that such theories are differentially applied to explain social problems among ethnic groups. First, the specific gene associated with various social problems has not been located. Also, for instance, white Americans have higher rates of teenage pregnancy, drug addiction, criminal involvement, and female-headed households than Europeans (Archer and Gartner 1983). But differences between Europeans and white Americans are always explained in terms of differences in cultural and environmental conditions (Oliver 1989). Why is one explanatory model used for whites but another for blacks?

The culture of poverty perspective argues that social disorganization, poverty, and inadequate socialization of children are the primary reasons for the high rates of social problems. Proponents of this perspective espouse the view that lower-class African Americans conform to a distinctive set of traditions and cultural values that condone involvement in problematic behavior (Banfield 1970; Oliver 1989). However, this perspective does not explain why only a small proportion of African Americans who experience poverty engage in behavioral patterns that indicate the internalization of norms in conflict with mainstream American norms (Oliver 1989).

Another explanation of social problems among African Americans is the racial oppression theory. These proponents argue that the majority of African Americans support mainstream values and goals, but "historical patterns of political disenfranchisement and systematic deprivation of equal access to educational and employment opportunities have induced a discontinued political and economic subjugation of Blacks" (Oliver 1989:16). Welsing (1974, 1978) discussed the inferiorization process. That is, the "systematic stress attack (involving the entire complex of political, legal, educational, economic, religious, military, and mass media institutions controlled by Whites) designed to produce dysfunctional patterns of behavior among Blacks in all areas of life" (Oliver 1979:21). In the inferiorization process, African Americans are conditioned to be functional inferiors. This means that blacks are socialized to be incapable of solving problems posed by the environment, while the inferiorization process is designed to enable whites to function as superiors.

Based on folk beliefs and folk/official research, media presentations perpetuate stereotypes of African Americans. Using Wolf's paradigm of power, the media is part of the power structure that orchestrates the production of images of African Americans. Walker describes the impact of stereotypes and overgeneralizations about Africa on minorities and nonminorities. In particular, she notes that we should examine not only why such negative images were created but, also why they continue to be taught in the schools. The educational system in America is used to maintain power relationships that existed since the European colonial exploration. To this end, the media collaborates with the educational system to maintain negative images of African-derived people. This is a significant part of the structural power that whites have to portray African Americans in various arenas.

Lyman (1990) provides an overview of how the movies portray people of African ancestry. He suggests that movies about African-derived people follow four basic themes:

1) the inherent superiority of Euro-American civilization, the white race, and colonial rule; 2) the sorrow and tragedy of interracial sex and/or marriage; 3) the loyalty and devotion of the African Servant; and 4) the altruistic service of white missionaries, doctors, engineers, and wildlife conservationists, who serve as models of civilization and tutors of modernity to grateful African natives. (Lyman 1990:50)

In the movies, dark-skinned women were relegated to three roles: (1) overweight or aged servants and confidantes to white families; (2) sensual temptresses who lured unsuspecting white men to depravity; and (3) fair-skinned tragic mulattos who suffered for their parents' transgression of racial mixing (Lyman 1990). Using the Great Chain of Being as the basis for their understanding of differences, the movies assigned dark-skinned people to the bottom of the linear chronology of geological and cultural time. Like anthropological texts, the movies showed a trajectory from savagery to barbarism to civilization. American movies have always lent support to European hegemony over dark-skinned people (Lyman 1990).

Jarvie (1978) believes that stereotyping is a defense against real and imagined threats. According to Lyman (1990) the stereotyping of dark-skinned persons as atavistic ape men, seducers of white men, and tragic mulattos reinforced white America's social beliefs. Myrdal (1944) pointed out that whites feared amalgamation with blacks and believed that black men wanted their women. A part of this apprehension was the white male belief in the sexual superiority of blacks and Africans and their fantasies about the presumed attractiveness of black men to white women (Lyman 1990:15). This was official in 1927 when Hollywood's Hays Office, which determined the sexual and violence content of movies, banned the cinematic presentation of romances between actors of different races. It also prohibited any positive images of intermarriage. As a result, blacks could not be feature players and ended up playing frustrated love objects in stereotyped dramas. Such characters lent support to a complex ideology of white sexual racism (Lyman 1990).

Besides the sexual-racist fantasies about black male threats to white sexual supremacy is the ambivalent lust-fear attached to the exotic black female. This ambivalence is based on the belief among whites that the ways of life in Africa, Pre-Columbian America, and the tropics are diametrically opposed to those of civilized Europeans (Lyman 1990). Allahar (1993) stated that those who are physically different are also assumed to be socially and culturally different and have different political and social beliefs. The movies used physical differences to impose stereotypical behavioral differences. They popularized racist stereotypes that were accepted by the average citizen.

The former's geo-temporal, physical, and cultural "otherhood" is said to be the source of a latent, perhaps sub-conscious, attraction (especially for white men) that, if allowed to emerge from its properly repressed place in the recesses of both the individual and the collective psyche, will lead to atavism and, eventually, to the destruction of Occidental civilization itself. (Lyman 1990:57)

Interracial sex must be avoided because white men must "take care not to contribute to the subversion of a civilization that has taken so many centuries and so much sexual abstemiousness to forge" (Lyman 1990:57).

While blacks in films were not allowed to love or marry their white "superiors," they were permitted to serve them faithfully and loyally. This hierarchy always positioned whites over blacks whenever they were in contact. We have all seen jungle, desert, and island set movies that present dark-skinned people as loyal servants. This reinforced the popular cultural belief in Europe's imperialistic and racial hierarchy. Whoopi Goldberg's movies continue the stereotype of the loyal servant.

Similar to other institutions of American popular culture, movies have been afflicted by what Gunnar Myrdal calls the "American Dilemma." This dilemma is the conflict between the American Creed, high national and Christian precepts, and group prejudice against persons different from whites where various impulses and habits dominate the white perspective. This also involves local social and economic interests and sexual jealousies. Through the movies, whites try to mesh national and Christian precepts with racist imagery and racially discriminatory acts against blacks (Lyman 1990).

These characterologies, together with the color of their anatomies, are inextricably connected to the cinematic thesis that black Americans are bound to an irremediably savage African past and consigned to an irrevocably demeaning American destiny. America's movies have built upon three centuries of stereotypical imagery to depict an Africa and Afro-America that is consistent with the society's deeply engrained cultural misinformation about the origins and future of dark-skinned people. In the process, they have elaborated on the myopic vision and embroidered upon a mass psychology of racism and cultural prejudice that shows few signs of being undone. (Lyman 1990:72)

Russell (991) stated that the movie *Birth of a Nation* exemplifies what she calls the "dominant gaze": "the tendency of mainstream culture to replicate, through narrative and imagery, racial inequalities and biases which exist throughout society" (Russell 1991:244). Russell derived the term *dominant gaze* from Laura Mulvey's (1975) feminist critique of Hollywood movies. There she suggested that popular films "serve the political function of subjugating female bodies and experiences to the interpretation and control of a heterosexual 'male gaze' " (Russell 1991:244). Russell uses the term *dominant gaze* to describe the process whereby American movies objectify and trivialize the racial experiences and identity of dark-skinned people, even when it purports to represent them. The power of the *dominant gaze* is in its projection of stereotypes and biases as truths (Russell 1991).

Black actors have to do the *Hollywood Shuffle*. That is, they must accept roles as drug addicts, pimps, and prostitutes, and they must conform to the negative images if they are to be employed. Racial stereotypes in American movies are as old as the movies.

the Tom (Edwin S. Porter's *Uncle Tom's Cabin*, 1903); the Coon (Thomas Alva Edison's *Ten Little Pickaninnies*, 1904); the Tragic Mulatto (*The Octoroon*, 1913); the Mammy (*Coontown Suffragettes*, 1914—a blackface version of Aristophanes' Lysistrata); and the Buck (*Birth of a Nation*, 1915) all inscribed on the nation's consciousness are cinematic images which persist to this day. (Russell 1991: 246)

The dominant gaze operates to perpetuate the subjugation of dark-skinned people in mainstream Hollywood films in three ways: (1) in the mass production of degrading stereotypes that dehumanize black history, experiences, and lives; (2) in the marginalization of indigenous views of black history, experiences, and lives; and (3) in the co-optation of racial themes in order to capitalize on the perceived trendiness of such perspectives. These trends usually overlap in the context of a particular film. For instance, Eddie Murphy's *Beverly Hills Cop* illustrated all three trends (Russell 1991). Whoopi Goldberg's movies also portray these trends, especially in regards to the loyal servant and caretaker of whites.

The last three chapters focus on interpretations of African Americans by African Americans. While Rhett Jones's chapter focuses on blackness as a physical and experiential concept that connects and unifies all people of a varied but similar phenotype, Page and Yvonne Jones examine African American responses to their blackness in the United States that were created by the one drop rule. For some, this response entails becoming like mainstream America, while others embrace a cultural nationalism in the tradition of W.E.B. Du Bois. As Rhett Jones points out, blacks are committed to the race concept although social scientists consider it invalid. Blackness means sharing history and experiences. Rhett Jones notes that "all black people were linked together by a shared experience in America's race-based slavery." Slavery shaped blackness. Race is a symbol of and reflects this common historical culture. It is a way to be a collective village in the spirit of nationalism. Blackness is also rooted in the awareness of slaves and free blacks that American society is based on untruths.

Given the continuation of this awareness, cultural nationalism, as portrayed by Yvonne Jones, provides a view of African-derived historical culture that may be outside of European-derived interpretations. Blacks are learning their cultural history and creating an African-derived identity through an inclusion of African-based historical involvements in local, national, and world developments. In this sense, producing a transnational African-derived identity.

An increasing number of scholars of African descent have promoted Afrocentricity as an intervention paradigm to help transform African Americans from a state of dependence to one of self-reliance (Asante 1980, 1987; Karenga 1977, 1986, 1988; Oliver 1989). From an Afrocentric perspective, the high prevalence of social problems among blacks is due to the imposition of a Eurocentric worldview on people of African descent (Oliver 1989). Karenga (1988) noted that Eurocentric socialization has had an adverse impact on blacks. Among other things it has produced self-hatred and depreciation of African people and culture and a loss of African cultural heritage, and has led to a Euro-American mode of assessing self, others, and the world. Afrocentricity encourages blacks to reclaim traditional African values and to transcend their cultural crisis. An Afrocentric worldview is not antiwhite, but facilitates the critical reconstruction of hidden parts of black self-formation and considers the African experience a legitimate paradigm of human liberation and human life (Karenga 1988; Oliver 1989).

In order to include the African worldview in the lives of African Americans, Afrocentric socialization must occur. The family, the educational system, the mass media, and the church are important in disseminating a group's cultural ideology. Afrocentric socialization is an interactive process in which parents and adults structure their behavior and institutions to promote the internalization of values that emphasize awareness of African cultural heritage and commitment to the economic and political development of people of African descent (Oliver 1989).

In *Songs of My People*, Page suggests that African-American entrepreneurs attempted not to provide an inclusive Afrocentric perspective to American life, but to submerge the African-derived social life in white Americanness. Isaacs (1963) found that prominent African Americans were ashamed of their ancestral homeland, and Reid (1972) and Davis and associates (1961) found that black students had no special interest in Africa or African affairs. This type of social discrimination by African Americans against Africans is more prevalent in urban than rural areas (Thornton and Taylor 1988). Page provides an example of African Americans becoming American by divesting themselves of their African heritage and denying the very existence of a heterogeneous African-American culture.

Both Page and Yvonne Jones discuss Africanness as a commodity. For Page, photographic images of African Americans were marketed like any other commodity. From that perspective, the African-American life was for sale but at a price. The price was a reconstruction of African-American existence to conform to the mainstream white-American model. The cultural nationalists also use Africanness as a commodity. For them, the selling of African clothes and other objects is a way to reaffirm their African origins. While these approaches may appear as opposites, it should be viewed as a continuum with most individuals floating between and at the ends at various moments in their lives. In both chapters, the authors suggest that African Americans are creating a racial identity in response to negative historical majority definitions of them.

ETHNIC/RACIAL IDENTITY

The self has many identities, including racial, ethnic, national, and community identities. The ethnic identity is part of the self which reflects shared symbols and meaning. These symbols and shared perceptions include positive stereotypes, perceived unique traits, and other social conventions of ethnic groups (White and Burke 1987). The key to ethnic identity is the internalization of meanings that are associated with an ethnic group (Burke 1980). In the photographic exhibit of *Songs of My People*, cultural nationalism, and Afrocentric entrepreneurship, African Americans are creating meaning associated with their African ancestry. In this sense, they are redefining their racial identity.

Membership in an ethnic group is usually ascribed and connotes a certain social identity (Goodenough 1969). Thus, ethnic identity is a cognitive process of social labeling (Ullah 1987). White and Burke (1987) examined ethnic identity among African-American and Anglo students and found that commitment to ethnic membership among African Americans was correlated with self-esteem. As the African-American identity increases, self-evaluation is also greater. Also, the more social contacts people have as a result of strong commitment to African-American ethnicity, the higher the self-esteem. Involvement with other African Americans creates a sense of security and self-worth (White and Burke 1987), as can be seen in Kwanzaa and the cultural study groups. To counter negative images in mainstream America, African Americans are increasing their self-esteem and commitment to racial identity by reading about the glory of Africa, Afrocentric entrepreneurship, and celebrating a newly created African-American holiday.

Safa (1968) discussed this process within a capitalistic system in Puerto Rico where those at the bottom (the poor) are an isolated social stratum. The poor reside in isolated residential areas where group solidarity becomes an adaptive response to their powerlessness (Safa 1968). A high degree of ethnic identity also is a response to an urban environment characterized by a great deal of heterogeneity and complexity (Eames and Goode 1977). Here strong ethnic commitment acts as a buffer against an insecure or unfamiliar environment. In Louisville, as elsewhere in the United States, African Americans need to feel secure. Strong commitment to ethnic identity, for example, Kwanzaa, is a way to create the perception of security.

BLACK RACIAL IDENTITY THEORY

Black racial identity theories began to appear in the psychotherapy and counseling psychology literature in the 1970s in response to the Civil Rights Movement. Counselors and psychotherapists wanted to be sensitive to racial issues that might influence the therapy process. Two major black racial identity theories appeared: the black client-as-problem (CAP) perspective and the Nigrescence or racial identity development (NRID) perspective. The Cap perspective attempted to explain inter-racial and intra-racial dynamics. With assimilation and demands by blacks that they be socially accepted, white American society was not accustomed to witnessing black leadership and assertion on a massive scale. Whites equated this assertion with aggression and whites believed that this hostility, violence and mistrust would be expressed in inter-racial interactions such as counseling and psychotherapy relationships. The CAP model suggested that certain overt behaviors would indicate which black clients were likely to be problematic for differing race of counselors (Helms, 1990a).

Vontress' (1971) typology proposes that there are three types of blacks: "black," "colored," and "negro." Each type was associated with certain intra- and inter-racial beliefs, feelings and behaviors. For instance, the "black" valued African physical appearance, was intolerant of whites, and understood the discrimination inflicted upon blacks. "Negroes" were integrationists who would accommodate blatant racism among whites while "colored" were blacks who evaluate and perceive themselves as whites do (Helms 1990a; Vontress 1971).

Creating a Racial Identity

What defines perspectives in client-as-problem models is their virtually exclusive focus on Black identity development as a consequence of societal pressures and their linking of clients' other-directed negative reactions (e.g., anger, hostility, rage) and behaviors to Black rather than assimilated identities or personality types. (Helms 1990a:10, 17)

Negrescence is the developmental process by which a person becomes Black. In this model black is defined in terms of mannerisms and evaluating oneself and one's reference group. Black identity is not defined by skin color. The model attempts to separate aspects of black identity development related to racial oppression from those that occur as a normal part of the self-actualization process. In NRID self-actualization was assumed to be expressed at the "most sophisticated level or type of racial identity development" while less sophisticated expressions were assumed to represent reactions to racial discrimination (Helms 1990a:17). Overidentification with whiteness was considered unhealthy and an attempt to survive in a racist culture. Theorists proposed that individuals could potentially move from least healthy, white-defined stages, to most healthy, self-defined racial identification. Each stage is a liberating metamorphisis of racial identity and symbolizes a psychologically healthier state of being. They use the idea of developmental stages to show movement of individuals from neative to positive self-ethnic identification (Helms 1990a).

In the NRID model it is believed that individuals sequentially move through the following four stages of racial self-identification: 1) the preencounter stage in which a person's worldview is dominated by a Euro-American perspective and a devaluation of blackness; 2) the encounter stage when an event(s) challenges the old perspective and causes the person to be receptive to a new interpretation of her/his identity; 3) in the immersion-emersion stage the person develops a sense of "Black Pride." However, at this stage internalization of positive attitudes towards one's blackness is minimal; and 4) internalization, the person internalizes a black identity and feels more satisfied with it. In this stage the person rejects racism but reestablishes relationships with individual whites who merit such relationships (Cross, 1971, 1978; Helms 1990a, 1990b; Parham and Helms 1981).

CAP and NRID were attempts by whites, i.e. white therapists, to predict black behavior and inter-racial interactions. The goal was one of predication. Currently, there is a grass-roots effort to redefine blackness by blacks. This effort is not for prediction but for spiritual and cultural solidarity and the affirmation of a positive racial self-identification. NRID assumes that one must sequentially move through the stages. I do not think this is true. For example, it is more likely that some people have always been in the third or fourth stage while never going through previous stages. Also, NRID assumes that blacks begin with a negative self-image. I do not think this is true either. Blacks can begin in any of the stages and do not have to move through them in a sequential order to attain a positive self-image or a worldview which does not condem all whites as evil.

African Americans vary in their attitudes toward black racial identity and vary in their public and private presentation of black racial identity. While the aforementioned attitudes exist, there may be another attitude, self-determination of black racial identity. African Americans are redefining blackness in light of a reclamation of their history, negative portrayals of blacks, and more opportunities to create/produce images about themselves for mass consumption. African Americans are determining what their image is and how it should be presented to the public. Self-determination of black racial identity is taking place among blacks and not those who simply want to categorize and predict their behavior.

CONCLUSIONS

bell hooks suggests that we must create counter-hegemonic art to combat the stigma of racism, sexism, classism, and other negative stereotypes. According to hooks, only counter-images can subvert the "dominant gaze" (hooks 1990; Russell 1991). African Americans must continually counter the "dominant gaze" if they are to have high self-esteem and, therefore, a positive racial identity.

This book is not an attempt to determine who should control the presentation of cultural and behavioral images of ethnic minorities, rather, it explores the motivation behind interpretations of African Americans by themselves and "others." It is hoped that this book will increase awareness and questioning of the motivation behind scientific investigations and interpretations by the majority who are phenotypically and culturally different from the group they investigate and write about. This does not mean that you must belong to the group in order to study them. Rather, you should be aware of racial as well as class and gender biases. Although this may seem obvious, those who usually do the interpretation, white America, do not take the depth of it seriously.

REFERENCES

Allahar, A.L. 1993. When Black First Became Worth Less. *International Journal of Comparative Sociology* 34(1–2): 39–55.

Archer, D. and Gartner R. 1983. *Violence and Crime in Cross National Perspective*. New Haven, Conn.: Yale University Press.

Asante, M. 1980. *Afrocentricity: The Theory of Social Change*. Buffalo, N.Y.: Amulefi Publishing Co.

———.1987. *The Afrocentric Idea*. Philadelphia: Temple University Press.

Banfield, E.C. 1970. *The Unheavenly City: The Nature and Future of Our Urban Crisis*. Boston, Mass.: Little, Brown and Company.

Burke, P. 1980. The Self: Measurement Implications from a Symbolic Interactionist Perspective. *Social Psychology Quarterly* 43: 18–29

Cross, W.E., Jr. 1971. The Negro-to-Black Conversion Experience: Toward a Psychology of Black Liberation. *Black World* 20(9): 13–27.

———. 1978. Models of Psychological Nigrescence: A Literature Review. *Journal of Black Psychology* 5(1): 13–31.

Foucault, M. 1984. The Subject of Power. In B. Wallis, ed., *Art after Modernism: Rethinking Representation*. Boston, Mass.: David R. Godine, pp. 417–432.

Davis, J., Hansen, R., and Burnor, D. 1961. *IIE Survey of the African Student: His Achievement and His Problems*. New York: Institute of International Education.

Eames, E. and Goode, J.G. 1977. *Anthropology of the City: An Introduction to Urban Anthropology*. Englewood Cliffs, N.J.: Prentice Hall.

Goodenough, W.H. 1969. Rethinking "status" and "role": Toward a General Model of the Cultural Organization of Social Relationships. In S.A. Tyler, ed., *Cognitive Anthropology*. New York: Holt, Rinehart and Winston, pp. 311-330.

Helms, J.E. 1990a. An overview of black racial identity theory. In J.E. Helms, ed., *Black and White Racial Identity*. New York: Greenwood Press.

———. 1990b. *Black and White Racial Identity*. New York: Greenwood Press.

hooks, b. 1990. *Yearning: Race, Gender, and Cultural Politics*. Boston: South End Press.

Isaacs, H. 1963. *The New World of Negro Americans*. New York: John Day.

Karenga, M. 1977. *Kwanzaa: Origin, Concepts, Practice*. Los Angeles: Kawaida Publications.

———. 1986. Social Ethics and the Black Family. *The Black Scholar* 17(5):41–54.

———. 1988. Black Studies and the Problematic of Paradigm—The Philosophical Dimension. *Journal of Black Studies* 18:395–414.

Lyman, S.M. 1990. Race, Sex, and Servitude: Images of Blacks in American Cinema. *International Journal of Politics, Culture, and Society* 4(1): 49–75.

Mulvey, L. 1975. Visual Pleasure and Narrative Cinema. *Screens* 16: 3.

Myrdal, G. 1944. *An American Dilemma*. New York: Harper and Brothers.

Oliver, W. 1989. Black Males and Social Problems: Prevention through Afrocentric Socialization. *Journal of Black Studies* 20(1):15–39.

Poussaint, A.F. 1983. The Mental Health Status of Blacks. In J.D. Williams, ed., *The State of Black America*. New York: National Urban League.

Reid, I. 1972. *Together Black Women*. New York: Emerson-Hall.

Russell, M.M. 1991. Race and the Dominant Gaze: Narratives of Law and Inequality in Popular Film. *Legal Studies Forum* 15(3): 243–254.

Safa, J. 1968. The Social Isolation of the Urban Poor: Life in a Puerto Rican Shanty Town. In I. Deutscher and E. Thompson, eds., *Among the Poor*. New York: Basic Books.

Thornton, M.C. and Taylor, R.J. 1988. Black American Perceptions of Black Africans. *Ethnic and Racial Studies* 11(2):139–150.

Ullah, P. 1987. Self-Definition and Psychological Group Formation in an Ethnic Minority. *British Journal of Social Psychology* 26: 17–23.

Vontress, C.E. 1971. *Counseling Negroes*. Boston: Houghton Mifflin.

Welsing, F. 1974. The Conspiracy to Make Black Males Inferior. *Ebony* 29:84–93.

———. 1978. Mental Health: Etiology and Process. In L. Gary, ed., *Mental Health: A Challenge in the Black Community*. Philadelphia: Dorrance.

White, C.L. and Burke, P.J. 1987. Ethnic Role Identity Among Black and White College Students. *Sociological Perspectives* 30:310–331.

Wolf, E.R. 1990. Distinguished Lecture: Facing Power—Old Insights, New Questions. *American Anthropologist* 92(3): 586–596.

Wright, G. 1985. *Life Behind the Veil: Blacks in Louisville, Kentucky*. Baton Rouge: Louisiana State University Press.
———. 1990. *Racial Violence in Kentucky*. Baton Rouge: Louisiana State University Press.

Index

Activist art: 80, 83
Africa: 27-47
African-American (Black) identity: 75-76, 87, 122, 145-147
Afrocentricity: 116, 135, 144, 148; cultural nationalism, 116; holiday, 120, 124, 130, 133; study group, 122, 125, 126, 133, 134

The Bell Curve: 15, 50
Binet, Alfred: 14
Biological determinism: 6, 8, 13, 16, 18-21
Black racial identity theory: 146-148
Blackness, definition, 49-51, 69-70; North America, 56-64; one drop rule, 51-56, 70; slavery, 64-69

CAP: *See* Client-as-problem
Client-as-problem: 146-147
Commodification: 76, 79; Africa, 131-133
Counter-identities: 90, 99, 100-102, 104, 107

Craniometry: 8
Cross-dislocation: 100-101
Cultural nationalism: 113-117, 134; afrocentricity, 144-145; entrepreneurship, 132-133; kwanzaa, 126-131; study groups, 126
Culture of poverty: 140-141

Diaspora: 28, 99, 106n.2, 108n.20, 113-117, 122, 126, 127, 129, 133, 134, 136
Dominant gaze: 143, 148

Entrepreneurship: 83, 90, 113, 145; Africa, 131-133; cultural nationalism, 116; ethnic identity, 146; kwanzaa, 127, 134
Ethnicity: 1-4, Africa, 63; ethnic identity, 145-146; definition, 49, 50; North America, 56, 57, 58, 61-64, 68-70

Films: Africa, 28-30, 32-42, 45, 81, 84, 86, 93, 107; Caribbean, 30-31, 33, 36; South America,

30-31, 33-34; United States 30-31, 36
Framework: See *History/Social Science Framework for Public Schools*

Gangsta rap: 102, 109n.22
Genetic inferiority: 140

Herrnstein, Richard:15, 50
History/Social Science Framework for Public Schools: 36-38, 41-42, 44, 46

Intelligence: 5, 8, 10, 14-15, 21-22, 50, 65
IQ: 9-10, 14-15, 22-23

Jensen, Arthur: 10, 14-15, 23
Jim Crow: 54-55, 73

Karenga, Ron: 113, 129-130, 135
Kwanzaa: 113, 117, 122, 124, 126-131, 133, 134

Murray, Charles: 15, 50
Museums: 1, 2, 76, 82, 83, 87, 101, 102, 104, 114

Nigrescence: 146-148
NRID: *See* nigrescence

One drop rule: blackness, 51-56; definition, 49-50, 63; slavery, 65, 68-70

Phrenology: 7, 23-24
Physiognomy: 7

r/k strategy: 5, 9-10, 19
Race: 7-14, 50
Racial oppression: 140-141, 147
Racism: 5-6, 8, 69, 76, 109n.20, 139-40; adaptive, 19-20; Africa, 28-39; 41; black racial identity theory, 146-148; blackness, 52-53; development, 16-19; films, 142-143; polite, 118; slavery, 60, 68
Reburial: 2
Rushton, Philippe: 5, 9-11, 23-24
entrepreneurship, 134; ethnicity, 57, 59, 60-63; kwanzaa, 130; one drop rule, 52, 54, 55

Social Darwinism: 8
Sociobiology: 5, 6, 9, 11-13, 18
Sociology of knowledge: 17-19
Spearman, Charles: 14
Stereotypes: 2, 5, 83, 140, 148; Africa, 28, 32, 35, 37-38; diaspora, 134; ethnic identity, 145; films, 141-143; one drop rule, 51; racism, 16

Visual activists: 76, 79-84, 86, 102, 104
Visual entrepreneurs: 76-77, 79-80, 82-83, 86, 90, 102, 104, 106
Voluntary association: 113, 117, 122, 125-127, 130, 132

White public space: 80, 85, 86, 102, 104, 105
Wolf, Eric:139-149

About the Editor and Contributors

Janis Faye Hutchinson received her bachelor and master degrees at the University of Alabama and her doctorate in Anthropology at Kansas University. She is currently associate professor in the Anthropology Department at the University of Houston. Dr. Hutchinson is a medical anthropologist who specializes in health issues among people of color. She has conducted research on hypertension in the Caribbean, biocultural research on condom use among African Americans, adherence to the tuberculosis regimen, and ethnographic analysis of changing relations between African Americans and immigrant Latin Americans.

Rhett S. Jones earned his B.A. "with Honors, and Distinction in Sociology" from the University of Illinois and did graduate work at the University of Connecticut, the University of Wisconsin, and Brown University, earning an M.A. in Sociology and an M.A. and Ph.D. in History. He is the author of more than two hundred scholarly articles, reviews, and essays; he has received grants from the American Council of Learned Societies, the Coolidge Research Colloquium, the Ford Foundation, the National Endowment for the Humanities, The Rockefeller Foundation, the Trotter Institute, and the Southern Fellowships Fund. Professor Jones's research interests center on the comparative study of race in the Americas before the 19th century.

Yvonne V. Jones is associate professor of Anthropology and chairperson of the Department of Pan African Studies at the University of Louisville. She conducts research on the entrepreneurial activities of African-American neighborhoods in Louisville, Kentucky. She edited (with Hans Baer), *African Americans in the South: Issues of Race, Class, and Gender* (1992).

D. France Olivieira is professor of anthropology in Surinam and a visiting professor in the Anthropology Department at the University of Massachusetts in Amherst.

Helán E. Page, associate professor of Anthropology at the University of Massachusetts in Amherst, Massachusetts, is a native of St. Louis, Missouri. She has served two terms as president of the Association of Black Anthropologists, a section of the American Anthropological Association. Dr. Page was the 1994-1995 Lilly Teaching Fellow. Her research interests include dialogic anthropology, American popular culture, nationalism, information-organizing behavior, and the politics of colonial and postcolonial race relations.

Jennifer Rasamimanana received her bachelor degree in anthropology at the College of William and Mary.

Sheila S. Walker, Ph.D., is currently director of the Center for African and African American Studies and is the Annabel Irion Worsham Centennial Professor in the Department of Anthropology at the University of Texas at Austin. Dr. Walker is an anthropologist and educator with more than twenty-five years of professional experience in Africa, Europe, Central and South America, the Caribbean, Asia, and the South Pacific. Dr. Walker was a member of the planning committee for the First Summit Meeting of African heads of state and African-American leaders held in Abidjan, Cote d'Ivoire, in April 1991, and is a member of the International Scientific and Technical Committee of the Slave Route Project of the UNESCO World Decade of Culture.

HARDCOVER BAR CODE